DATE DUE

Jack London

JACK LONDON

the Man, the Writer, the Rebel

ROBERT BARLTROP

Pluto  Press

First published 1976 by Pluto Press Limited
Unit 10 Spencer Court, 7 Chalcot Road, London NW1 8LH

Copyright © Pluto Press 1976
ISBN 0 904383 18 0

Designed by Tom Sullivan

Typeset by Red Lion Setters, Holborn, London
Printed in Great Britain by
Lowe & Brydone Printers Limited, Thetford, Norfolk

B
1. London, Jack
2. title

Contents

We would like to thank the
Jack London Room, Oakland Public Library and
the Bancroft Library, University of California,
for permission to use the illustrations
on the following pages.

Jack London the schoolboy, in Oakland, 1887

The seal-hunter 'Sophia Sutherland'

Illustration from 'The Call of the Wild,'
first published 1893

Jack in the Klondike, 1898

Anna Strunsky

Jack London with his husky
'Brown Wolf' in 1905

Jack London
Piedmont
Alameda Co., Calif.

April 24/03

Dear Anna:— This is the first
writing I have done for some
time. Easter Sunday I elected
to cut off the end of my
thumb, and not finding
the piece, have had a
painful wound to heal

Mabel applegarth has been
spending a couple of weeks
with us —— likewise
Cloudesley Johns.

Am glad you liked the
dog story. Have a heart beating
in the end of my thumb,
so ——

Jack London.

Letter from Jack to Anna Strunsky

Bess London about 1900, in their home

2268 East 15th Street, Oakland, where Jack and Bess lived after their marriage

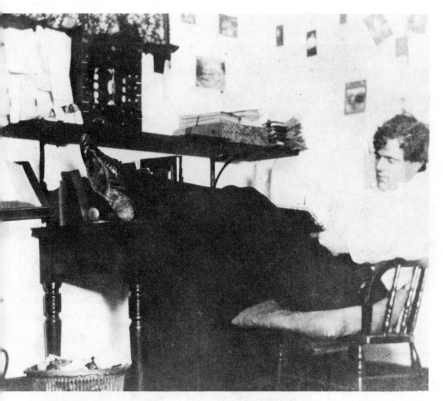

Jack in his study, 1900

Jack with his two daughters, Bess and Joan, 1905

Salvation Army Barracks, in
the East End of London, from
'People of the Abyss,' first
published 1903

Jack London during his
lecture tour of 1905

Jack and Charmian, shortly after their marriage

Before the 'Snark' sailed: James Hopper, Charmian, George Sterling and Jack

The 'Snark' crew in the South Seas. In the centre: Charmian, Jack and Martin Johnson

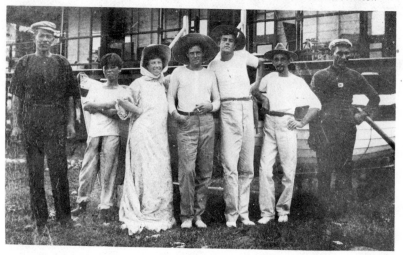

Jack and Charmian on the ranch-house porch

George Sterling, James Hopper,
Harry Leon Wilson and Jack at
the Bohemian Grove, 1913

Also in the Bohemian Grove,
Jack London on the right

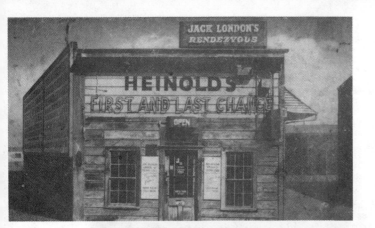

The First and Last Chance Saloon, Oakland

The ruins of the Wolf House

Architect's drawing of the Wolf House

*Charmian in front of the
ranch-house, 1930*

Charmian in the 1920s

Jack London in his study

Commemorative plaque and sculpture, Jack London Square, Oakland, by Jack's friend, Finn Haakon Frolich

Jack London shortly before his death in 1916

Foreword

I first heard of Jack London when I was nine years old. In our town's new talking super-cinema they showed a trailer of *The Sea Wolf*, coming shortly. The author's name in huge rugged letters; waves crashing; a tough-looking unkempt man standing in a lurching cabin, his shirt agape. I never saw the film — it was the Alfred Santell version, and there had previously been silent ones — but an image of Jack London was created for me.

Two years later I read an account of the heavyweight fight between Jack Johnson and Jim Jeffries at Reno in 1910. It began with how Jack London had demanded in the press that Jeffries should be brought out of his six-year retirement to 'wipe the golden smile off the nigger's face', and ended with the old champion's frightful defeat. In between, I found that London was a writer of Alaskan stories and had been there himself in the gold rush. The picture of the man in the cabin expanded. He was associated with red-blooded true adventures like those in the *Wide World* magazine; he was truculent and prejudiced, pushing his bare chest forward. I liked the stories — *White Fang, The Call of the Wild, Burning Daylight* — but not him.

Then, in my teens, I discovered him as a socialist writer. One of my friends had a passion for his works. We talked about *The Iron Heel* and *The Jacket*, while I was fascinated by *The Road* and its wonderful beginning: 'There is a woman in the state of Nevada to whom I once lied continuously, consistently and shamelessly for the matter of a couple of hours.' I started collecting the books in second-hand shops, and went on doing so over the years. Occasionally I came across lavish American copies — once I picked up *When God Laughs* in the handsome Sonoma edition, lent it, and never got it back; but mostly they were blue-covered ones from the cheap, serviceable Mills and Boon publication of all Jack London's works in the nineteen-twenties. Now and again I found foreign editions as well: *Les Vagabonds du Rail, Il Richiamo della Foresta, Colmillo Blanco.*

The contradictions of the man abounded. Beside his vigorous, compassionate crusading for the working class I had to view the assertive, near-vindictive racialism; beside his insistence on hard logic — 'the fact, the irrefragable fact' — the embarrassments of trite sentimental stories. I searched for years for a copy of *The Kempton-Wace Letters*, of which Jack London was so proud. One afternoon in a bookshop in Glasgow I told my companion, Joe Richmond, about it: when I had finished explaining he said 'If you want it so badly I'll give it to you'. It was pretentious and empty, a handful of prejudices and intellectual postures.

As time went by, however, I came to know and I think to understand Jack London. Judgements such as that he was a prophet, a revolutionary or a fascist, or the archetype of American individualism, leave nearly every question unanswered. Better guides to understanding were had, in fact, from meeting and listening to men who had shared his background. Charles Lestor was one of them; his lecture on Jack London culminated in a thundering recitation of the poem from *The Iron Heel*:

> The man you drove from Eden's grove
> Was I, my Lord, was I,
> And I shall be there when the earth and the air
> Are rent from sea to sky ...

Lestor had adventured and taken part in political life in North America early in the century. His talk, not particularly informative in itself, communicated the flavour of Jack London and his time.

Three full biographies have been written. They are his wife's two-volume work, Irving Stone's *Sailor on Horseback*, and his daughter Joan's. All are invaluable, each is restricted. Charmian London's story of her husband is told in terms of his relationship with her. Most readers would find it cloying and too heavily charged with Jack's subjectivism, though its greatest failing is its omissions and concealments; nevertheless it contains a mass of material about his life. *Sailor on Horseback* is a popular biography without pretensions to being anything else or to evaluating his ideas and writing. Part of its intention was to give names and facts Charmian had passed over and to show her in a less warm light.

Joan London's book is the outstanding one of the three, yet it virtually excludes personal relationships. The reasons are clear enough. The child of her father's short first marriage, she knew little at first hand that was lovable or even pleasant about him; her observations are a feat of careful objectivity. Her book is concerned with the social history of Jack London's lifetime, the economic growth of America, the philosophical ideas and the political movements which were the waves on which he rode.

All these books are American. As far as I know, no study of him beyond prefaces and reviews has been produced in England. Yet Jack London's books have appeared, and remain in print, in every language and country. Lenin had *Love of Life* read to him on his deathbed. *The Call of the Wild* and *White Fang* are children's classics everywhere. In some of the Mills and Boon editions, the list of his books had asterisks beside those which had been made into films: the number is astonishing. Periodically I am told by booksellers that Jack London is 'coming back', but he has never been away very much. The strength of his appeal was once shown vividly to me when I was a teacher in London, a number of years ago. I read his story 'The Mexican' to a class one afternoon. At its improbable, marvellous climax — the youth's moment of victory against all odds, and his vision of guns for the revolution as he stands exhausted — the fists of fourteen-year-old boys and girls silently pounded in relief and exultation.

There is, then, every reason for a book seeking to view Jack London as writer, socialist and whatever else, and man; and that has been my aim. I have described his upbringing and early years without dwelling on them, since detailed accounts and homely incidents are to be found in other works, Charmian's in particular. On the other hand, there is a good deal of material not included in any previous work. The fact that this book is written near the centenary of Jack London's birth is coincidence, not deliberate timing. However, it suggests an appropriate time for assessment and, it should be said, for celebration. For he was a remarkable man. He created for millions a world of adventure that was not fantasy but scenes from his own life, and dramatised some of the theories of the young socialist movement.

I have used the word 'socialist' indiscriminately for an assortment of people and ideas, because that is how it was used at the beginning of the century. Today we should recognise many of them as liberals, reformists and, in some cases, worse things; at that stage, few questions were being asked. Apart from the obstructions that would be caused in the text, it is impossible to explore all the instances. It is a fact that socialists today get knowledge and inspiration from books by men who became, or probably would have become, capitalist politicians and supporters of Communist dictatorships. While therefore leaving 'socialist' at its face value, I draw the reader's attention to the chapters in which Jack London's socialism is discussed.

No bibliography is given because I doubt its value for the general reader. A list of books and articles dealing with Jack London appears in Philip Foner's political anthology *Jack London, American Rebel* (Citadel Press, New York, 1947); and there is Woodbridge, London and Tweney's *Jack London: A Bibliography*, published by Talisman Press, Georgetown, California, in 1966. A further addition to the works named is Franklin Walker's *Jack London and the Klondike*, published in Britain by The Bodley Head. However, I have given a list of Jack London's own books and their contents, so that stories which appear in collections with other titles can be located. Some recent editions in Britain and other countries have re-grouped his stories and short pieces; references in this book are to the original publications.

My gratitude must be expressed to people who have helped me. I am indebted to Anne and Arthur Lipow of Berkeley, California, for invaluable help in finding illustrations and for information about Joan London; I. Rab of Newton, Mass., for supplying a copy of Jack London's letter to the Workers' Socialist Party; Edgar Hardy, for information about Ernest Hunter; Harry Young, for his reminiscence of Edmundo Peluso; Mr Edmund Cork of Hughes Massie Ltd. for telling me about Jack and Charmian London's association with his firm; Charles P. Davis of New York for a letter on 'General' Coxey, and S.E.Parker for a letter on Benjamin De Casseres; and the American Library of the University of London, to whom no enquiry was too much trouble. Bill Christopher, Israel Renson and Robert Murray lent books to me. I wish specially to thank the publishers who, once the idea of the book was hatched, gave tremendous encouragement and help.

In addition, many friends have played a part. Over the years, countless conversations and exchanges of opinion about Jack London directed my attention to fresh aspects and contributed to an understanding of him. Almost certainly, without them this book would never have been written.

1. Boyhood That Never Was

Jack London was born in San Francisco on 12 January 1876. His wife's biography of him[1] published in 1921, five years after his death, gives an account of his parents and their circumstances. His father, John London, had been a farmer in Iowa. Widowed and left with a large family, he sold the farm and became a contractor in San Francisco. There he joined a spiritualist circle and met Flora Wellman. They married, and Jack was their only child. Soon afterwards John London's business failed. He was a canvasser for a time, then took his family across the Bay and became a smallholder again at Oakland, to which Jack always referred as his Home Town.

It was not until 1938 that a different story was told. Irving Stone's *Sailor on Horseback* began with an account from the *San Francisco Chronicle* in June 1875, of Flora Wellman's attempted suicide. She had been living with 'Professor' W.H.Chaney, a travelling Irish astrologer and a man of many mistresses. On her telling him that she was pregnant, there had been a quarrel — the *Chronicle*'s story was that Chaney had 'driven her from home for refusing to destroy her unborn infant'. Flora went to the house of William H. Slocum, a journalist for the *Chronicle*, and remained there until the child's birth; she gave lectures on spiritualism and denounced Chaney. Whether she met John London before or after the birth of her son is unknown, but they were married on 7 September 1876 and she signed her name 'Flora Chaney' on the marriage licence.

The same version appeared in *Jack London and his Times*, by Jack's daughter Joan London, published in 1939. She spoke of William Chaney's six marriages, remarking that little happiness resulted from any of them and there was 'little doubt that few of his many marriages were legal'. After describing him she said: 'This was the man who, at fifty-three, and to spite his wife, made Flora Wellman the fourth Mrs Chaney.' Despite the ambiguity, there is no doubt at all that Flora was not married to Chaney; she could hardly have married John London so shortly afterwards had that been the case. They had a short-term liaison which ended, as attested by the *Chronicle*'s story, on 3 June 1875 and which according to Chaney began less than a year before. Joan London's account is confidently written, with no hint of any uncertainty as to her father's parentage. And Stone reprints the notice which appeared in the *Chronicle* on 14 January 1876: 'Chaney. — In this city, January 12, the wife of W.H.Chaney, a son.'

Jack was aware that Chaney was reputed to be his father, but failed to make certain of it. A person of a later generation would seek and accept proof or disproof from official records, as Stone did. However, these were less obviously accessible at the beginning of the century. In 1897, when he was twenty-one, Jack London wrote to Chaney asking him directly and indicating a desire for 'silence and secrecy'. Chaney's reply denied it. Addressing Jack as 'Dear Sir', he wrote: 'I was never married to Flora Wellman, but she lived with me from 11 June 1874, until 3 June 1875. I was impotent at that time, the result of hardship, privation, and too much brain work. Therefore I cannot be your father, nor am I sure who your father is.'

Chaney continued that the episode, particularly through the *Chronicle* report, had brought disgrace and unhappiness to him: all his relatives except one sister had refused to have any more to do with him. He said he had published a pamphlet, supported by the police, refuting the 'slanders' that he turned Flora Wellman out of doors because she had refused to have an abortion. He ended: 'I am past seventy-six, and quite poor.' Jack wrote again, pressing his enquiry, and in a final reply Chaney described Flora's suicide attempt as a sham and repeated that he was impotent. (Irving Stone suggests that this was a confusion of words; he meant not that he and Flora had never had sexual relations, but that he believed himself sterile and unable to create a child.) He implied that Flora had been with other men. What Chaney's letters convey is his strong wish not to become involved.

It is almost certain that Charmian London knew and was

concealing. Her account of John London's early life is full of details, but it becomes indefinite after his widowhood — 'early in the 'seventies' — and about what happened in San Francisco. The circumstances and duration of his courtship of Flora are disposed of in a single half-sentence: John 'wasted no time in binding to him his desire'. Most significantly, the date of their marriage is not given. Even if Charmian lacked verification of the Chaney story, the dates would have shown Jack London to be illegitimate.

The desire to show good breeding and a sturdy background was paramount in Charmian. Evidence suggests that other people were aware of this in her. In 1924 Adolph Kohn, a well-known figure in the socialist movement on both sides of the Atlantic, referred in the *Socialist Standard* (London) to the 'bourgeois lady' who had misrepresented her husband's outlook; he had this view of her from American associates. The opening chapter in her book is headed 'Heredity'. It speaks of 'pride of race', quickly dissociates from a Jewish line of Londons, and names Sir William London who fought with Washington as Jack's ancestor. Flora Wellman likewise was of good Welsh stock, her family in America since before the Revolution.

In fact Jack's father, William Chaney, was an exceptional man. Both Irving Stone and Joan London believed that there was a striking physical resemblance between him and Jack. Chaney was short, sturdily built and vigorous. The doctor who attended Flora during her pregnancy is said to have recognised Jack London, at sixteen, as Chaney's son. To attribute adventurousness, intellectual power and financial irresponsibility to the relationship depends on one's view of heredity; nevertheless, both men had them. What is known about Chaney is due to his writings, which had a good deal of autobiography in them.

He was born in 1821 in New England, where his father was a prosperous farmer. The farm was sold when he was nine, his father having died after an accident, and William Chaney was bound to a neighbouring farmer. His mind on books and studies, he ran away and worked sporadically at manual jobs. He went to sea for a time, eventually joined the navy, quickly deserted. He wrote stories and novels, became an advocate — unsuccessful, it is said, because he inveighed against the dishonesty of courts and lawyers. There were bankruptcies, and the first of his several marriages. Politics interested him.

In 1866, Chaney met Dr Broughton in New York and was converted immediately to astrology. The period was one in which beliefs spread like wildfire in American cities — religious revivalism, utopian socialism, women's emancipation, spiritualism. While astrologers and mediums flourished, the New York papers were attacking them and their meetings were fair game for hooligans. After a quarrel, Chaney found himself in prison for twenty-eight weeks — having tried to have the law stop a disrupter, he was charged with bringing about a false arrest. He won over a woman prisoner to astrology, and married her in December 1867. However, a year later he parted from her and went off lecturing in the north-west. He was about to return to New York towards the end of 1873 when, in San Francisco, his pocket was picked and he had to stay. He spoke on and practised astrology throughout the winter. To him it was an exact science like mathematics and physics, and his lectures were full of entertaining erudition.

By Chaney's own account he was preparing again for the journey to New York in the spring of 1874 when he had a letter from his wife. In it, she said she was divorced and could re-marry but — presumably by some legal provision — if he married again she would have him imprisoned. 'This roused my ire', and in June 1874 he took another wife: Flora Wellman. She joined him at 314 Bush Street, which was his home and office, and a little later they moved to 122 First Avenue. She helped at his meetings, selling literature on astrology. Chaney also wrote for *Common Sense, a Journal of Live Ideas,* which William Slocum edited. It was a magazine in which political radicalism rubbed shoulders with every other kind of unorthodoxy — free love, diet reform, spiritualism and astrology. There was a considerable overlap among these veins of thought, and the general feeling that they were all subversive of tradition and the established order led their enthusiasts to support one another and to receive Chaney favourably in their circles.

The favour ended abruptly, however, when he rejected Flora. Slocum and his associate in *Common Sense,* Mrs Amanda, befriended her and attacked him; it can be surmised that Slocum was responsible for the vehemence of the *Chronicle*'s article. Chaney left San Francisco. For some years he lived with his sister at Portland, publishing and lecturing. After a spell in New Orleans he ended in Chicago where he married Daisy, the last Mrs Chaney, and described himself as Principal of the College of Astronomy. He died in poverty, selling one-dollar horoscopes, at the time when his son Jack London was becoming world-famous.

Flora Wellman too was a person out of the ordinary. Much younger than Chaney — she was born in 1843, and thirty when she went to live with him — she was a tiny woman, less than five feet tall. Her grand-daughter Joan recalled her speaking of going to balls and parties during the Civil War; she had been brought up in some luxury, but ran away from home at sixteen and in 1874 made a living by giving piano lessons. At some time as a young woman she had typhoid fever, which ruined her looks. She had bad eyesight and wore a wig because much of her hair had been lost through the fever. That she was unstable and melancholic may or may not have been also due to illness. Her mother died when she was a baby, and she was said to have been a petulant and difficult child.

Chaney alleged that Flora was promiscuous. What can be said, at least, is that in San Francisco she found an environment where unconventionality was acceptable. She made friends among the 'progressives', and was able to practise the spiritualist beliefs to which she had taken. However, as an older woman she said little about her earlier life, and kept few friends who might have known anything of it. She aged rapidly after her affair with Chaney and her son's birth, but her self-will and instability were dominant factors in the London family's life.

Flora's physical weakness made it impossible for her to feed the infant Jack, and a wet-nurse was employed. This was a black woman who had lost her own child, Mrs Prentiss. She had been born a slave in Virginia, and sold apart from her mother as a small child. She became 'Mammy Jenny' to Jack; she doted on him and remained an important background figure throughout his life. In his babyhood an English couple, looking for a child to adopt, went to her house and asked to see him. Her account, related years afterwards to Charmian London, described how she had dressed-down her husband for letting them through the doorway; and ended with confessing herself to have been heartbroken when she had to wean the baby from her breast.

The Londons lived for a year in a cottage at Bernal Heights in San Francisco, while John London canvassed for the J.M.Flaven

Company's IXL Emporium. He improved his income by going to the Singer Sewing Machine Company as general agent and collector, and the family moved to a six-room flat in Folsom Street. This was one of several former mansions which, before their destruction by the fire of 1906, had been split into apartments or become boarding-houses. Flora found another home before long, a house in an attractive corner at the end of Natoma Street; the family might have stayed there longer but for an epidemic of diphtheria.

Jack, still a baby, and his sister Eliza both caught the disease. Flora nursed them determinedly — Eliza remembered in later life having heard her mother asking whether they could be buried in a single coffin to save money should the worst happen. They recovered, but the doctor suggested convalescence in the country. This revived John London's hankering to be a farmer once more. He found a home and a piece of land in Oakland, a suburb of San Francisco. His plan was to grow vegetables, particularly tomatoes, and sell them from a shop at 'The Point', the junction of Seventh and Campbell Streets.

Jack London described his foster-father as 'too intrinsically good to get ahead in the soulless scramble for a living that a man must cope with if he would survive in our anarchical capitalist system'. Obviously John London had a great deal of optimism but little business sense. His business was developed by hard work, compromised by honesty and ruined by trust. He took a partner named Stowell to run the shop while he worked and canvassed for orders. After a week-end trip, he found he had been robbed lock stock and barrel by Stowell. He went to law in search of restitution, but ended with only a few dollars. Beginning again on his piece of land — it adjoined the race track at Emeryville, Oakland — he raised vegetables.

The Londons moved to various homes in Oakland. When the business was on its feet again they changed to a fifteen-acre farm in Alameda, and John expanded it by taking in strips of the neighbouring flats. The mothering of little Jack was done largely by his sister Eliza. In San Francisco she wheeled him in his perambulator, at Alameda she took him to school with her. The teacher gave him a box for a desk and picture-books to look at; this is probably the explanation of his being able to say later that he could read and write at the age of five without recollecting being taught to do either.

Flora was continually restless, unable to stay in any home or give her attention to anything besides spiritualism for long. Jack's strongest impressions of his childhood were to be of loneliness and insecurity; he was left with a hatred of country life. His mother had schemes of all kinds. She sold gold-leaf for picture-framing, started a kindergarten, sold lottery tickets. Séances were held in the house; when Jack was six he was made to take part in them. And there were the scenes and tensions which a neurotic person can generate. In one of them Jack heard for the first time of Professor Chaney, if not by name. The notes he made in adult life for an autobiography (to have been called 'Sailor on Horseback') include a six-year-old boy overhearing his parents quarrel; the father reproach the mother for having a baseborn child; and the mother crying 'I was so young, and he promised me a bed of roses'.

Mammy Jenny moved to a cottage near Alameda, and Jack spent a good deal of his time playing, eating and being nursed there. He played with Mammy's own half-white children, and it seems surprising that he grew up to hold violent convictions about the inferiority of coloured people. However, Flora Wellman had stiff racial pride which must have been communicated to him early. She was fond of boasting that she and hers were of 'old American stock' and not 'dagoes' or other immigrants — indeed, part of Jack's loneliness was being kept apart, on the ground of superiority, from Irish and Italian neighbours. And Mammy Jenny would have shared those sentiments. Her pride was in being a full-blooded negress; she was a strongly religious woman who valued her position in the community, which almost certainly included taking for granted that white ruled over black.

Jack and his sister Eliza went to the West End School, Alameda. Eliza read to him at bedtimes, and described him as always having a book in his hand and loving stories. Though he was physically sturdy, loneliness and shyness intensified his addiction to books. Those which impressed him greatly as a boy were Washington Irving's *The Alhambra*, a life of Garfield, and Ouida's *Signa*. He declared through his life that the last of these had more influence on him than any other book. He identified himself with the Italian peasant boy who became a famous musician; and

Ouida's romantic, half-rebellious philosophy sank deep into his mind.

When he was eight, the family moved again. This time it was to a larger farm at Livermore. John London started with vines and orchards, but at the end of a year was persuaded to build ambitious facilities for chickens. Calamities followed. Not the least was that Eliza, now seventeen and given charge of the chickens, married and left. Her husband was a middle-aged widower named James Shepard, who with his three sons had been boarding with the Londons. The bank to which John London had mortgaged his farm foreclosed, and he acknowledged defeat at last. In 1886 they returned to Oakland, taking a large house in Seventeenth Street. Here Flora too made her last venture. She attempted to make it a boarding house for women cotton-mill workers. When it failed, John's occupations became those which denote a retired man: deputy constable, special officer, watchman.

The move provided Jack with what mattered most: access to a public library. It was a ramshackle wooden building next to the old City Hall in Fourteenth Street. The eleven-year-old had Eliza's family — they lived not far from the Londons' new home — as well as his own apply for tickets for his use. He roused the interest of the librarian, Miss Ina Coolbrith.[2] After he had gone through books which were sophisticated as well as weighty (he read Wilkie Collins's *The New Magdalen* and the unexpurgated works of Smollett) she began to guide him. It was his first contact with a cultured person, and Jack was fascinated as well as grateful. Finding that his greatest enjoyment was books of travel, adventure and discovery, she supplied everything she could. He read obsessively, continually exciting his emotions; he demanded to be left alone, and developed nervous jerks.

He was delivering newspapers to earn money for the family because John London was in and out of work. He had to get up in the dark each morning, and deliver more papers after school; he was paid twelve dollars a month, of which Flora allowed him to keep ten cents a week. He augmented it by a little trading with rag-and-bone merchants, and saved his money for dramas and operas at Dietz's Opera House and the Tivoli. The latter had been a family treat on Saturdays when they were at Alameda. Charmian London knew of its wonders as a child, but was not allowed to go;

she heard about it from her relatives' talk, while 'Johnny London actually, with his own rounded orbs, beheld the absorbing spectacle'.

The newspaper round and other occupations made him part of the street and dockside life of Oakland. Shabby and solitary, he sought every odd job and opportunity to scrape more money. Ten years later he wrote to Mabel Applegarth, his first sweetheart:

> I was eight years old when I put on my first undershirt made at or bought at a store. Duty! — at ten years I was on the street selling newspapers. Every cent was turned over to my people, and I went to school in constant shame of the hats, shoes, clothes I wore. Duty — from then on, I had no childhood. Up at three o'clock in the morning to carry papers. When that was finished I did not go home but continued on to school. School out, my evening papers. Saturday I worked on an ice wagon; Sunday I went to a bowling alley and set up pins for drunken Dutchmen. Duty — I turned over every cent and went dressed like a scarecrow.

He was responding warmly to reproaches by her. It was almost all true; but his indignation made him omit what he gained from that time. The dreams of adventure that books had brought him were given verification. These were the final years of the great age of sail. Oakland Estuary had boats from all over the world. In the winter the Arctic whalers lay in the Bay. There were the smaller craft, each one with its own aura of romance and excitement — fishermen, oyster-pirates, Chinese and Japanese craft, smugglers and curio-hunters. Jack saw the life of saloons and dives, drunkenness and violence, and listened to the sailors' yarns and talk. The sea drew him like a magnet.

In one respect only the letter was untrue. He did not let Flora know all the things he did or give her all the money he earned. Spending more and more of what time he had to spare round the Yacht Club on the Estuary, he scrubbed decks and did other jobs on the boats while learning all he could of how to sail them; and hoarded the cents he earned to buy a boat of his own. When he was thirteen he had it, for two dollars. It was old and leaky, but he ran it up and down the Estuary and even in the Bay, capsizing and colliding as he taught himself to master it.

By the time he left school, at thirteen, home had become to Jack simply a place where he handed over money, ate and slept. He was not without affection for his parents. From John London he had a quiet companionship at times; but that gentle, dreaming man was not the sort who could impose his personality against the chaos created by Flora's. In later life Jack recalled to a friend, Henry Mead Bland, that he had rejected Flora's authority because of an unjust punishment, but another reason was her persistence with spiritualism. Before he was twelve he habitually escaped from the house when séances were arranged or her 'fits' — trances in which she spoke to the spirits of Indian chiefs — began; and the legacy he obtained from them was a lifelong scorn for all religion.

He was chosen to take part in the school-leavers' ceremonies but stayed away because of his shabby, ill-fitting clothes. No trade or career was suggested to him. John had nothing to pass on, and Flora either could not bring herself to contemplate the matter or was satisfied that he continue newspaper-selling and doing odd jobs. He went on thus for another two years. He acquired a fourteen-foot skiff and spent days at a time on it, again concealing earnings to buy paint, a sail and oars. He went out regularly into the Bay now, as far as Goat Island, took home fish, and became a skilful small-boat sailor. He took books with him from the public library, covering them with newspapers to keep them dry.

The expeditions intensified his solitude. Just as he sailed alone, he read and thought alone without sharing or discussing whatever was unfolded to him. According to Charmian he would say to her of his youthful struggles: 'No one has helped me vitally — name me one.' Many other people could say the same, with the same degree of truth. Jack London's case was that of a boy isolated by his family's circumstances, whose early passions for reading and physical adventure led to further being alone in different senses.

However, the adventurous life he sought required a certain camaraderie; and from this need an incident came that had much significance for the future. He made the acquaintance of a run-away English sailor named Scotty, who was full of tales of deep seas. 'Here was a man,' Jack wrote later, 'looking on critically, I was sure, who knew more in one second about boats and the water than I could ever know.' Scotty took the tiller of Jack's skiff — and, his time spent in the forecastles of big ships, was incapable of sailing her. After nearly capsizing, he ran the skiff full tilt into the wharf and shattered her nose.

But Scotty took Jack aboard the yacht *Idler* which lay near the whalers in the creek. The *Idler* was said to be interned for smuggling opium from the Sandwich Islands; its caretaker was a bronzed nineteen-year-old, waiting for a berth as a harpooner on one of the whaling ships. On board were all the seafaring paraphernalia — oilskins, sea-boots, charts and signal flags, and a calendar pinned to the wall with mariners' dividers. And then came the drink. The two youths produced cheap fire-water — 'blind pig'; fourteen-year-old Jack poured the burning stuff down his throat, keeping pace with his companions until all three were thoroughly drunk.

While the other two lay stupefied, he fell into the skiff and careered across towards Oakland, singing at the top of his voice. The tide was out; he foundered in mud a long way from the boat-landing, tried to punt with an oar, and collapsed into the slime where a broken pile gashed him. The next two or three days were all sickness and misery, trailing round with the newspapers, struggling at odd jobs: and vowing, as he was to vow often, that he would never drink again. There remained also a feeling of pride. He had sat with two men to whom this was a familiar game, matched them and in the end beaten them at it.

At fifteen, the life of the streets and boats ended abruptly for him. The family's fortunes had gone still further downhill. They were living in an old cottage near the Estuary, among dilapidated shacks. John London, who had been working irregularly as a watchman, was injured in an accident; Jack had to go to work to earn more money. He got a job in Hickmott's cannery in Myrtle Street, West Oakland. The building was an abandoned stable, insanitary and draughty, and here he bent over unguarded machinery for a basic ten-hour day at ten cents an hour. There were a number of boys and girls there. Accidents involving the loss of fingers were frequent. The others dared not look when it happened — inattention to the machines would mean the same for them. Jack later recollected, too, the dirt which continually dropped into the cans of fruit.

Because money was acutely needed at home he worked the longest hours that were physically possible: at times eighteen or twenty hours at a stretch. He said he once worked at his machine for thirty-six hours continuously, and sometimes earned fifty dollars a month. It was almost all turned over to his mother. He walked to and from work, and slept perhaps five hours a night before Flora pulled his bedclothes off to awaken him. His existence was that of a work-beast, made still more loathsome by the wretchedness of the home. There was no time or energy for reading or sailing now. He hoarded the few cents allowed him from his wages, telling himself he would buy a skiff to replace the battered old one. After several months he had five dollars: one day Flora, desperate for money, went to the machine where he stood and asked for it.

The time in the cannery, and its conclusion, were to be the material of an outstanding short story — 'The Apostate'. Jack walked out. First he spent a day in his boat on the Bay, where he had not been for what seemed a lifetime. He thought over his situation: he did not know a horse in Oakland that worked as he did, and he was still only fifteen. Unlike the boy in his story, he accepted that he must go on providing for his family. What he must do was escape from the numbing, dehumanising toil of the factory. He wanted to be at sea, and did not care if it meant drunkenness or law-breaking so long as he could earn money. He was ready for what Charmian called 'an equally pernicious but more attractive abyss'.

Oyster piracy had been established for several years in San Francisco Bay. Californian oysters were despised until, after the building of the transcontinental railroad, seed and yearlings of the prized Atlantic varieties were transplanted to the mud flats of the Bay. The railroads themselves took over the beds and sold them at high prices; by 1890, one or two companies controlled the industry. Piracy was a natural outcome. The pirates came from Europe, Scandinavia and the Mediterranean as well as America. They had to be skilful small-boat sailors, and courageous to the point of recklessness. They were at the mercy of armed watchmen and the Fish Patrol; their other enemy, chosen by themselves, was the Chinese fishermen whom they attacked wantonly. They drank and brawled, and many came to violent ends. But the prizes were enticing: boatloads of oysters to sell to merchants on the city wharf at dawn.

Jack made brief enquiries into the piracy business. He calculated how much he might make — he had formed the habit two or three years before of writing down income and expenditure. And then he learned that French Frank, a man of fifty with much notoriety, wanted to sell his sloop *Razzle Dazzle* for three hundred dollars. Determined that it must be his, Jack went to his old nurse, Mammy Jenny Prentiss; her home had remained his occasional refuge where warmth could always be found. He asked if she could lend him the money. She had been working as a nurse, and handed it to him unhesitatingly in twenty-dollar gold pieces. A couple of days later, on Sunday, he rowed out to the *Razzle Dazzle*, made certain of his purchase, and joined a party gulping down red wine: French Frank, Whisky Bob, Spider Healey and two girls named Mamie and Tess. Next morning the agreement was drawn up and signed. Jack London was master of his own craft, his home now a little cabin that smelled of tobacco, 'red paint' — thick, vile leavings from wine-vats — and romance. He was an oyster pirate.

It is tempting to say that he had finished with childhood and become a man. It would not be true, however. If such a line were desired it could as well be drawn when he began to traipse the Oakland streets selling papers, or when he entered the cannery. The *Razzle Dazzle* took him into a fraternity of men, where sexual experience, hard drinking and brutal adventure at once became parts of his life. But the truth is that Jack had scarcely known childhood. Isolated, given little affection other than Mammy Jenny's; driven to pleasures as well as work that were grown people's; carrying family responsibilities and calculating debits and credits — he was an adult at ten years old. In his 'duty' letter to Mabel Applegarth he said 'I had no childhood', and later: 'I never had a boyhood, and I seem to be hunting for that lost boyhood.'

2. The Dignity of Work

The title Jack was proud of for the rest of his life, Prince of the Oyster Pirates, arose because Mamie — the Queen — moved in to make him the only skipper with a woman aboard. On his first day on the *Razzle Dazzle*, the day of the party, she made love to him on the cabin roof; when he became owner of the boat, she took for granted that she would stay there with him.

She was sixteen, and hitherto had been French Frank's girl. 'Mamie' was Jack's fiction-name for her. At the time he told Charmian about his life with her he revealed that he had received his sexual initiation earlier, from 'one much older than myself'. There is no other reference to this woman, and the likelihood is that she was someone met in in his tours of the Oakland streets and saloons. Mamie was attracted by his youth and vitality, fresh as they must have seemed after French Frank. She was pretty, and mature beyond her years — a waterside waif for whom childhood had quickly given place to worldly wisdom. She made a home for the two of them in the tiny cabin, while French Frank lay in jealous rage.

On his first night as master of the *Razzle Dazzle*, Jack took part in his first raid. The twenty-year-old wharf-rat Spider Healey had become his crew; they joined a flotilla which included Big George, Young Scratch Nelson — son of Old Scratch, named after he had clawed the faces half-off men in brawls — Clam, and Nicky the Greek. They were all armed with revolvers. When they reached the oyster beds they filled one sack after another, and at dawn Jack raced with the others for the morning trade. One night's work had brought him as much as three months in the cannery.

He repaid part of Mammy Jenny's loan at once, and handed most of the rest to Flora. More such nights followed, with adventures and more money than he had dreamed of. French Frank, whose jealousy he had dismissed unbelievingly, tried to run him down in a squall — Jack held his course, working the wheel with his feet while he pointed a double-barrelled shotgun to make the Frenchman keep his distance. One night he brought in the *Razzle Dazzle* with the biggest load in the pirate fleet. Another time, in the dawn race for the first and best of the morning trade, Jack's craft arrived first without a rudder. And he was still barely sixteen, the youngest of them all.

With the loan paid back in full and his family provided for, inevitably he drank heavily. He was readily accepted for his seamanship and his fearlessness, but the standing of a man among men required him to drink to excess. Jack disliked the taste of liquor and the memory of what it had done to him previously, but he was determined to outdo his new comrades at this as at everything else. One of his proudest moments was on learning that the story of a bout with one of the waterfront's greatest drinkers had gone round: he had been 'soused all afternoon with Old Scratch'.

The place for all the waterfront men was Johnny Heinhold's First and Last Chance Saloon in Webster Street. Jack first entered it on the Monday morning when he bought the *Razzle Dazzle* from French Frank; one foot on the sawdust floor and the other on the brass rail, he tossed down whiskeys with the rest of them. Heinhold became his friend in the months of oyster-pirating, warning him when he had had enough (and at other times, when money was short, giving him credit). One night's carousing cost Jack a hundred and fifty dollars. Yet he still took adventure books from Miss Coolbrith's library and lay for hours reading them in his cabin.

Then the *Razzle Dazzle* was wantonly destroyed. The accounts are brief and varied; they involve a brawling, drinking orgy of all the fleet on the sand-flats opposite the Oakland waterfront, and the burning of the boat's mainsail by Scotty. Jack does not appear to have given an explanation to Charmian. In fact he seems to have started a phase of destructiveness, caring little about anything. There is no means of knowing whether it began suddenly or developed from piracy and drinking: biographers' phrases like 'months passed' can deceive. We do not know how he parted from the Queen, or what the truth about most of the events was. When Jack and Charmian met Scotty in Melbourne in 1909 he insisted that it had been Jack who burned the mainsail.

A possible explanation is that the other pirates, or most of them, turned on Jack. His subsequent fame led to recollections of him being romanticised; he gave a retrospective rosy sheen to his youthful drinking in *John Barleycorn*. He had an appealing personality and good looks, but without doubt also he was precocious and intent on showing himself to be top dog. It is significant that the man he went off with after the fight, Young Scratch Nelson, had been injured in it, and in Jack's accounts of the ensuing months there is no further mention of the rest of the pirate fleet. The abandoned *Razzle Dazzle* was raided, dismantled and set adrift by a rival oyster-pirate gang — or were they Jack's ex-comrades, running him off their territory?

At any rate, the destructiveness remained in the period which followed. He went into partnership with Nelson on the latter's *Reindeer*; broke, they borrowed money for stores from Johnny Heinhold. (The remains of the *Razzle Dazzle*, when Jack recovered them, were sold for twenty dollars.) Though he always spoke of his time with Nelson as a period of high adventure, he was now going downhill. On the *Reindeer* they sailed wildly from one end of the Bay to the other. They acted as if courting death, steering to miss destruction by half-an-inch, going out into dangerous tides. Jack no longer supported his family. The money he and Nelson made went on extended, violent drinking bouts which became the talk of the Bay. One night they joined a political rally for free whiskey; Jack awoke next day, after being beaten up as well as drunk, in a waterfront lodging-house.

Both of them were bored now. Nelson decided to return to Oakland; he was dead in less than two years, shot through the head. Jack stayed at Benicia, loafing and drinking, earning a little money fishing for salmon. After a time he became a deputy of the Fish Patrol, apparently because he had fallen in with other patrolmen, but the sequence of events is again imprecise. In a letter in 1903, telling an editor the experiences from which *Tales of the Fish Patrol* came, he said: 'later on, this Nelson and myself, in the *Reindeer*, were up in Benicia with a load of oysters, when we were approached by one of the Fish Patrolmen with a proposition which took our fancy, and for some months afterward the *Reindeer*, Nelson, and myself, took an active part in the raids on the law-breaking fishermen.' But Nelson does not appear in other reminiscences of this period, and it seems that Jack was re-arranging and rationalising it.

The deputyship was not an official post in any sense. There were patrolmen proper, appointed and paid salaries by the state board, but the deputies were free-lances whose pay was a percentage — possibly half — of the fines collected from lawbreakers. The Fish Patrol was started in 1883. Its purpose was to check the decrease in salmon and other fish round the Californian coast, but its underlying concern was the Chinese immigrant problem. A Fish Commission report in 1886 estimated that nearly two thousand Chinese were engaged in fishing, mainly for shrimp and sturgeon, about San Francisco Bay. Most illegal fishing was attributed to them, and Chinese appear repeatedly as villains in Jack's stories. The law-breaking included oyster-piracy as well, however; and Jack's complaisance in readily turning to law enforcement must again raise the question whether he had drifted away from the pirate community or been placed at odds with it.

Though he was sailing the Bay again, and knowing excitement, the existence was sporadic and undisciplined. He still spent much of his time drinking in waterfront saloons. He claimed to have once been drunk for three weeks on end: 'I mean, literally, that I did not draw one single, sober breath for twenty-one days and nights.' The debauch led him to attempt suicide. At one o'clock one night, trying to board his sloop at Benicia pier, he fell into the water. A strong current swept him towards the sea; surrendering to it, he decided that he would let himself drown. To help the process, at Dead Man's Island he got rid of his clothes and swam so that he was not caught on the piles of the steamboat wharf. In mid-channel he lay back in the water, looking at the stars and singing, full of self-pity. The cold water gradually restored some sobriety, and before dawn the boy's mood had changed to near-panic at the thought of drowning. It was almost too late — he was exhausted and swallowing water — when a passing fisherman saw him and hauled him out.

His demoralisation intensified after the episode. He left the Fish Patrol and wandered back to Oakland. On his way he met a group of 'road kids', young hobos, bathing in the river at Sacramento. They were characteristically hard-boiled youths with similar backgrounds to his own, from poverty-stricken or otherwise unattractive homes and unwilling to accept the toil and restraint of industrial jobs. Jack stayed with them a few weeks. They christened him 'Sailor Kid', and he picked up their lore and vocabulary. Then he moved on, seeking the familiar waterfront. In Oakland he saw Nelson again, but they had little in common now other than the desire for a drink.

Except for odd jobs he did no work, and fell in with gangs of hooligans who roamed the West Oakland streets. Later in his life he dismissed this phase as illustrating only the vicious herding of people in cities, but it represented the pattern he had fallen into at the time. Indeed, he failed to integrate himself even with gang life: he was, as his daughter wrote, 'unable to become a part of the rank and file of any group'. The isolation to which he had accustomed himself had made him unsocial. On one hand he dreamed of conquests — and he had mastered whatever he attempted — but, on the other, he could not accept or perhaps even comprehend the requirements of social intercourse among equals.

He went on drinking when he had the money, and might easily have been killed in waterfront brawling — in the kind of life he led, men often were. He saw his family occasionally. They were in a cottage at Clinton Station; it was one of a cluster built from the timbers of demolished buildings at Badger Park, where Jack had worked in the bowling alley (the district appears as 'Weasel Park' in *Martin Eden*). Then, near the end of 1892, he pulled himself together suddenly. There may have been something which is unrecorded, but what is most likely is that he saw the unloveliness of his situation and the need to break away. There was a sealing fleet wintering in San Francisco Bay, and he cultivated the men's company. One of the hunters, Pete Holt, promised to take Jack as his boat-puller. On his seventeenth birthday he signed on a beautiful three-topmast schooner which he called *Sophie Sutherland*. A few days afterwards he was aboard going through the Golden Gate, heading for the coast of Japan and the Bering Sea.

The *Sophie Sutherland* (her name appears in the official register of merchant ships as Sophia Sutherland) carried no liquor, and wages were to be paid at the end of the seven months' voyage. Despite lacking any experience of bigger ships, he had signed on as an able-bodied seaman; he was confident that he would learn in no time. Nevertheless, he acted warily. He sensed some contempt for his youth, and he knew that false steps or ineptitude would reduce his status among the other A.B.s to that of a doormat.

At the same time, he was aware of being more knowledgeable and more adaptable than most of them — and able, if it came to it, to hold his own in a fight. If they were watching him critically, he must keep one jump ahead of them all the time. He did his work well, and felt the barriers breaking down. He listened to arguments which came to blows, avoiding involvement in them. However, the incident which won for him acceptance was a fight with a giant Swede called Red John.

The Swede was more of a bully than the rest, continually looking for trouble. It was his peggy-day, his turn at cleaning the sailors' quarters; Jack sat on his bunk making a rope-yarn mat to take back for Eliza. Red John called out an order to Jack and, when it was not obeyed, struck him across the face. Jack flew at him; the others scrambled into their bunks to watch. Dodging the huge swinging fists, Jack wrestled his way on to the other's shoulders, locked legs round his throat, and — perhaps remembering Old Scratch — drove his fingers into the Swede's eyes and windpipe. His opponent butted him into the deck beams again and again, lacerating his head and shoulders. But the gouging fingers won, and Red John had to give in while Jack screamed: 'Will y'leave me be? *Will* yuh? *Will* yuh?'

From that time he was one of them: 'It was my pride that I was taken as an equal, in spirit as well as fact. From then on, everything was beautiful, and the voyage promised to be a happy one.' And so it turned out. They saw no land for fifty-one days until they arrived at the Bonin Islands (now called Ogasawara Jima), where sealing ships stopped for water and repairs before going northwards for the hunting. Jack was thrilled and delighted. Canoes and sampans in the harbour, and a view of mountains surrounded by tropical vegetation: it was everything his library-books had promised. With a Swedish sailor named Victor and a Norwegian named Axel he made plans to spend their ten days in port exploring, fishing, and climbing the mountains.

But first they would have one drink — just one. As of all the previous times, Jack was to say: 'I did want to be a good fellow and a good comrade.' They never reached the mountains and palm trees. Instead, their time was spent soaking up saké and adulterated whiskey, with the tiny doll-like Japanese courtesans. One night he and his companions wrecked a house of entertainment, crashing through the paper walls. Hoping to stop this sort of thing, the authorities were trying to have all seamen returned to their ships by sunset; Jack ended under the stars with a crowd of apprentices from the Canadian sealers and was left, stripped and drunk, on the doorstep of the Japanese port-pilot's wife.

When they left the Bonin Islands there were three months' strenuous work. Their place on the sealing grounds found, Jack pulled the oars in the hunters' boats in the grey, foggy Bering waters, and took his part in skinning seals and salting the hides. The deck every day was like a slaughterhouse, covered with fat and blood, the men competing in the numbers they had ready to be salted down at the end of the season. The brutality of the occupation produced brutal fun. Several of them hauled a skinned monster of a seal into the forecastle and laid it in the bunk of Long John, who always slept naked. They lay and watched him pull off his clothes and vault in to be pressed against the slimy, bloody carcass; beside himself with rage, Long John tried to fight the whole forecastle.

With a heavy catch, the *Sophie Sutherland* pulled in at Yokohama on her way home. It was the biggest city Jack had ever seen, with huge docks and modern buildings everywhere and a population of nearly a quarter of a million; all the more astonishing because the Californians' image of Japanese and Chinese alike derived from Mongolian laundrymen, cooks and coolies, half-comic and half-sinister immigrants from backward regions. The *Sophie Sutherland* was made spick and spotless before any man was allowed in port. Then they were released. They found rickshaws and made for a Japanese saloon. The fortnight in Yokohama was like the ten days in the Bonin Islands; Jack saw nothing beyond the sailors' drinking places. One exploit earned him a few days' fame. Chased by the port police, he dived into the harbour and swam a mile back to the *Sophie Sutherland*. The police registered him as drowned, and were awe-stricken when they saw him again next day.

As they sailed back to San Francisco, Jack's mind was made up on what he would do. The months on the voyage had been therapeutic. His demoralisation had been arrested; he was fitter and stronger and felt more alive than at any time before. He had done a lot of reading on the voyage, having taken a pile of books from the library and from Miss Coolbrith's own collection. With a tiny light held in one hand, while the rest of the crew slept he read Melville, Flaubert, and *Anna Karenina*. Pete Holt wanted Jack to join him as boat-puller again on the *Mary Thomas*, but Jack excused himself. (The *Mary Thomas* put to sea in due course, and was never heard of again.)

He left his mates drinking away their wages and took the ferryboat home to Oakland. John London was in poor health and the family in debt. Jack bought a second-hand coat, waistcoat and hat, and some cheap shirts and underwear, and handed over the rest of his pay. His aim was to settle down: find a job, and study. Times were bad, however. 1893 was a depression year in the United States, and unemployment was widespread. The only work he could find was at a machine in a jute mill — for ten cents an hour, the same wage he had earned in the cannery at fifteen. And, as then, there was no choice: the money was desperately needed.

There was no resentment in Jack's mind over his work-situation. In his essay 'How I became a Socialist', published in 1905, he said 'orthodox bourgeois ethics' had dominated his thinking: 'The dignity of labour was to me the most impressive thing in the world. Without having read Carlyle, or Kipling, I formulated a gospel of work which put theirs in the shade. Work was everything. It was sanctification and salvation.' He was, of course, dramatising, but undoubtedly he took pride in his capacity for physical work. He seems to have been seeking satisfaction in conformity. He went to the YMCA for the companionship of serious-minded boys, and — almost perversely, in contrast with Mamie the Queen and the little Japanese girls — had a sugary, shy boy-and-girl friendship formed at a Salvation Army meeting.

In this unlikely phase, when he was trying to accustom himself to a different kind of life, Jack wrote his first piece and had it published; and it came from the recent old life. The San Francisco *Morning Call* had been running competitions for amateur writers.

Flora noticed an announcement offering twenty-five dollars for the best descriptive article. Why it gave her the idea that Jack should enter is not easy to see. Perhaps she recalled Professor Chaney's fluency with his pen; or perhaps she thought simply of the twenty-five dollars. She pressed him persistently, suggesting that he write about something he had seen while on the *Sophie Sutherland* voyage. Jack was unenthusiastic at first — after thirteen hours a day in the jute mill he came home tired. Then he remembered an episode: he was still at the kitchen table writing at breakfast time.

The competition entries were limited to 2,000 words. Jack wrote 4,000; he spent another evening cutting down, and yet another making a fair copy. Flora, whose venture this was, took charge of the manuscript and delivered it to the *Call* office. 'Story of a Typhoon off the Coast of Japan, by John London aged 17' won the first prize, by the unanimous decision of five judges. Their collective verdict in the *Call* was: 'The most striking thing is the largeness of grasp and steady force of expression that shows the young artist.' The second and third prizes were won by students at the universities of Stanford and California.

The article was published in the *Call* on 12 November 1893 — edited, and probably robbed of vitality, by the judges' recommendation that Jack's present tense be changed throughout to the past tense. It remains strong and vivid today; everything described in it was fresh in Jack's memory. John and Flora London were delighted. John bought a pile of copies of the *Call*, Flora was full of glee at the success of her scheme. Jack was tremendously excited. His dream of being like the hero of *Signa* came to life. He spent more evenings at the kitchen table writing another story of sea adventure and sent it to the *Call*. However, the editor had no use for this kind of material after the competition, and sent the manuscript back.

It is worth considering the sources of this remarkable, unexpected success. As a child he had a passionate fondness for stories, and was said to have been good at describing events he had seen. He maintained that the impetus to writing had begun for him through an incident at school when he was twelve. He found himself at odds with the music teacher; she sent him to the principal, Mr Garlick, who ordered that in future he spend the music periods writing compositions. Whether or not it was intended as a retribution or reproach, its effect must have been invaluable.

But, principally, his reading had given him a rich vocabulary and shown possibilities for imaginative expression that had so far remained in storage. Nor had they been subjected in his mind to any critical direction. Had he received a higher education he would have been directed towards a conventional 'good prose style'; he might have been told that his beloved Ouida was trash, that Jacobs[3] and other writers he admired were not material for serious attention. In that sense Jack London was more fortunate than he knew. He acquired materials of language and experience which were those a clamorous changing America, by-passing academic tradition, was almost ready for.

For the moment, however, his anticipations quickly faded. His notebook for this time shows thirty cents spent on stamps and envelopes, indicating that he tried other publications. Then, apparently thinking the effort hopeless, he resigned himself to the mill. Conditions there were almost as bad as those in the cannery: deafening daylong noise, the air full of fibres, and machines worked by crippled and consumptive children. He had given up the YMCA, finding its earnest young men pallid after the company he had known. On Sunday afternoons he walked the streets with a friend named Louis Shattuck, looking for girls.

In this respect, Jack felt himself unsophisticated. He was sexually experienced, but did not at all know girls as Louis did — how to win their attention and talk engagingly to them. He was envious of his friend's self-assurance that enabled him to raise his hat to a pretty girl and walk off down the street with her. Jack's longing for something of the sort led to the love-affair he had at this period. It consisted of sending notes, sitting tongue-tied in the park, exchanging a few innocent kisses, before the girl's visit to the city ended. Yet the past was never far away. One night he was stopped by a woman he knew — Charmian believed it might have been the Queen — who had news to tell him: she had seen Young Scratch die.

He had been promised a rise to $1.25 a day at the jute mill. It did not materialise, and Jack looked for some way to better himself: learn a trade, perhaps. He thought of learning about electricity, and went to the superintendent of the power plant for the Oakland street railway. Jack explained his wish, and emphasised that he was willing to start at the bottom. In later recollection he named the man as Grimm: a huge important man with white sidewhiskers. He was engaged, and put to shovelling coal for thirty dollars a month.

He slaved at it, strapping up the small wrists which were always weak in comparison with the rest of his physique. He would fall asleep on the streetcar going home and again over his supper, so that John and Flora carried him to bed many nights. After several weeks he learned the truth. He had taken the place of two men, each paid forty dollars a month, who had thrown over the work because it was too much for them together. Jack held the job a little longer, to prove it could not defeat him, and then resigned; he went home and slept for twenty-four hours without waking.

His efforts to settle down and conform had failed. He had found no opportunity to study and no direction to take. The doubts and unhappiness were returning. He felt a revulsion from labour of the sort he had been doing (indeed, the coal-shovelling had condemned him to wearing wrist-straps for more than a year). It is possible too that he began drinking once more. In *The Cup of Fury*, an attack on alcohol published in 1957, Upton Sinclair referred to Jack's having begun 'industrial drinking' when he was at work after his pirating and sealing adventures. The chronology is scrappy, deriving from a dinner-table account Jack gave in 1905, and Sinclair associates the industrial drinking — 'When Saturday night came, he was utterly exhausted and *wanted* to get drunk' — with a period in a steam-laundry two years later. Perhaps it was true of both times; the desire to break from each phase seemed to follow too much drink.

At any rate, Jack was ready to sheer off again. He walked along the waterfront and thought how he might get to sea. No doubt he would have done so but for something else which caught his attention. It was April, 1894. The industrial depression had become still worse, and an army of the unemployed was being organised to march to Washington. In several American cities detachments were being formed under self-styled 'generals': one in Los Angeles, and another in San Francisco. In Oakland, leadership was taken over by a compositor and labour activist named Charles Kelly. He was demanding free railway transport to Sacramento for his followers; it was the kind of opportunity Jack wanted, for different associations and to see the cities of the east side of America. With ten dollars given him by Eliza, he hurried to join the train.

3. On the Road

The unemployed armies were protest movements representing one aspect of the desperation caused by the depression. Agriculture as well as industry was at a standstill; banks had closed; there were 35,000 out of work in San Francisco alone. The armies had the support of the angry and impoverished farmers, strengthened further by the common hatred of the Southern Pacific.

Their political demands were those of the Populist party formed in 1892, and were given dramatic expression in the bizarre figure of Jacob Coxey and his 'good roads' campaign. A stone-quarry proprietor from Massillon, Ohio, Coxey was preoccupied with ideas of currency reform — in 1876 he left the Democratic Party, accusing it of having 'sold out to Wall Street', and in 1885 stood unsuccessfully for the Ohio legislature with an inflationist programme. He was brought to the new Populist party by Carl Browne, who besides political crusading was given to a religious theory in which Christ was reincarnated in chosen human beings.

Thus, the official title of Coxey's Army was 'The Commonweal of Christ', and its form and paraphernalia were from Browne's imagination: leaders on horseback, banners, the catchphrase 'petition on boots'. However, 'good roads' was Coxey's own plan for ending unemployment. The demand was for Congress to issue $500 millions in paper money, at the rate of twenty millions a month, for the building of roads all over the United States. The unemployed would provide the labour-force. They would be paid a dollar and a half an hour, the working day limited to eight hours; thus the pump would be primed for a revival that, if this policy were retained, would never end.

The doctrine was an early version of Keynes's thesis that the weapon against depressions was public spending, on projects of social utility, on pyramid building, even for the government to 'fill old bottles with banknotes, bury them at suitable depths in disused coal-mines ... and leave it to private enterprise on well-tried principles of *laissez-faire* to dig the notes up again'. Persuaded by Browne, the American Federation of Labor endorsed the 'good roads' scheme, but Coxey remained an unsuccessful minor figure in American politics; he died, still agitating, at ninety-seven in 1951. His theory left its impression on Jack London, however — in the economics of the Oligarchy's rule in *The Iron Heel*.

Jack went to join General Kelly's train at the scheduled time of seven in the morning, and found himself left behind. There had been an alarm in the night, and an attempt to arrest Kelly; all the men available had been bundled into boxcars bound for Sacramento. Using some of the money Eliza had given him, Jack took a passenger train and arrived at Sacramento to find that the army had left on another train for Ogden. Recalling what he had learned from the road-kids two years before, he and a companion named Frank Davis jumped on the Overland train and 'held her down' — rode illegally — until they were thrown off. They aimed for another after dark; Frank caught it, but Jack was left behind and caught another going to Reno.

Here he saw another unemployed detachment forming. Wanting to catch up with his friend and with Kelly's Army, he pressed on. He rode 'blinds', the mail-cars without end doors where tramps could cling to the platform-boards, and 'went underneath' on the rods under the trains. On one blind, in the space behind the coal-car, a spark set fire to his clothes; at forty miles an hour he had to tear off his overcoat and jacket and throw them away.

He caught up with Frank at Winnemuka, and they boarded another train. Then Frank gave up. Jack kept a diary of this time: 'The Road has no more charms for Frank. The romance and adventure are gone and nothing remains but the stern reality of the hardships to be endured.' There were large numbers of others heading eastward to join the eventual meeting of the armies. There were also gangs of hobos — 'the profesh', the aristocracy of the road whose acceptance Jack wanted most of all. Off the trains he 'threw his feet', 'panhandled', 'battered the main stem': the terms for begging and scrounging. In fact he was able to obtain food relatively easily because of widespread sympathy for the unemployed.

Ten days after he left Oakland Jack boarded a refrigerator car in a blizzard on the Rockies. Eighty-four men were lying on straw inside it; they were the rearguard of Kelly's Army. One of them recalled him as a young man with 'round features and curly hair', wearing a cap and a fur coat with a book in each pocket. He said he was known as Sailor Jack but — since he was required to enlist formally in the Army — his name was Jack London. He was introduced to his comrades through the 'threshing machine', being thrown back and forth from one recumbent man to another, the length of the car and back.

They rode on through the blizzard, telling yarns and full of good humour. When they reached the Nevada plains they wired to the authorities of Grand Island that they would be arriving; there they were taken to restaurants, given meals, and marched back. Then they reached Omaha, where they disembarked, at one in the morning. They were shipped across the river to Council Bluffs under police supervision, and from there they had a six miles' walk to where Kelly's Army lay in Chautauqua Park.

It was pouring with rain. Jack and a Swede sought shelter for the rest of the night in an empty saloon; it was bitterly cold, and he lay under the bar shivering in his wet clothes until daylight. After begging his breakfast and the fare to ride to Chautauqua Park, he saw Kelly's Army — camped in mud, soaked, huddled round smoky fires. There were sixteen hundred of them. Jack discovered that the estimate of him as 'about twenty' was fortunate. The army had a stipulated lower age-limit of twenty, and he saw an eighteen-year-old ordered home: Jack was not yet eighteen and a half.

That day the army moved on to Weston and then towards Des Moines, with Kelly on horseback at the head. They were now more than two-thirds of the way to Washington; public sympathy remained strong, but the authorities' attitude was hardening. Further railway transport was refused, and the trains were guarded by Pinkerton men. There was no choice but to continue marching. Jack's feet were severely blistered. He hitched rides and continually petitioned the commissary for a pair of shoes; when he got them they made matters worse. Other men were in as bad a state. Jack took to 'throwing his feet', disappearing from the column for hours to return loaded with the fruits of begging expeditions.

On the march, and sitting round fires at night, they talked. This was where Jack London first heard socialism being expounded and discussed. Like all demonstrations of its sort, the army of the unemployed was made up principally of working men in whom radical consciousness had already been roused. A high proportion were trade unionists, to whom the idea of showing unity in the class struggle was as important as Coxey's economic plan. From their talk of books and theories of society Jack was given a new perspective on his experiences in the cannery and the power-station. Listening, he saw the position of the working class as a trap from which he had to escape.

By the end of ten days' journey to Des Moines, the good spirits of the army were fading away. There had been quarrels among the leaders, with a San Francisco socialist named George Speed disputing Kelly's authority and criticising his conduct. The men were footsore and exhausted; they voted to stay where they were until transport was provided. The railways were adamant. The authorities fed nearly two thousand men for several days and let them sleep in a disused factory. The army lounged in the sun; Jack joined in games of baseball.

When eventually they moved, the inspiration came from the Populist party leader General Weaver. They would take to the Des Moines river on rafts, which would carry them into the Mississippi and thence to the Ohio river, to within a few hundred miles of the American capital. Local labour leaders organised the supply of materials and carpenters. When the first rafts were put on the river, Jack's title 'Sailor Jack' led inevitably to his being given charge of one of them. His experience and skill quickly put him and his nine-man crew ahead of all the rest, and his proficiency at begging and scrounging brought them the best of the countryside's pickings. In a short time the other crews were angry and Kelly was sending orders for them to drop back. They were christened 'pirates' — a familiar and not unacceptable name to Jack; while they lived well on food, coffee and tobacco, the army following behind went hungry.

At last Kelly sent two men on horseback to tell the farmers and cottagers that the army disowned these scavengers. The warning was effective. Jack and his crew were forced back to the main contingent, and were refused food. Nor can it be disputed that the others' anger was justified. The picture of a glorious lark, in which initiative and ability were reaping their reward, leaves out that it took place at everyone else's expense. The doctrine of the survival of the fittest, which was to be a dominant theme in Jack's stories, was already affirmed in his outlook. Loyalty, which he extolled to Charmian as the greatest of virtues, was always over-ridden by his conviction that he would be top dog and the weaker others would go to the wall.

The army was increasingly demoralised and desertions were taking place now. Discipline could not be stringent or lasting. Within a couple of days Jack was again at the front, this time in company with one of Kelly's lieutenants on a double raft. There were twenty men to row, and they were able to move at almost the speed of a steamboat. Others imitated them in joining pairs of rafts, and raced against them. When they reached the Mississippi a monster raft was made by lashing several together. For a little over twenty miles they floated in this manner through Tom Sawyer's country. Then Jack picked up a letter from his mother. He had written home a week before, and her reply told him that a few dollars had been mailed to Chicago Post Office for him.

On 24 May, probably the night he received this, he wrote in his diary: 'We went supperless to bed. Am going to pull out in the morning. I can't stand starvation.' They were at Hannibal, Missouri. Early next day he and a few others took a skiff, which they left in turn for holding down trains, gradually parting company. Jack arrived in Chicago on 29 May; he dropped off a cattle train at seven in the morning. Deserting the army required no justification. The unemployed movement had been disintegrating for a month or more, and its remaining optimism had collapsed when the news came of General Coxey's débâcle in Washington. Accompanied by only a small contingent, Coxey was arrested for walking on the White House lawns; for a generation, any rag-tag crowd in eastern America was called 'Coxey's army'.

Jack was tempted, no doubt, by the news that a little money was waiting for him and a reminder that some of Flora's relatives in Michigan were ready to welcome him. Apart from this there was the fact, made plain by the raft episode, that he would fare better as a tramp on his individual resources than as one of a crowd. Plodding on for a nebulous objective had no appeal to him — he had joined in any case for his own reasons, not because he identified himself with the unemployed and their demands; but what he had seen of the road-kid life attracted him strongly.

There were five dollar bills in the mail at Chicago Post Office. He bought some second-hand clothes from 'the Jews of South Clark Street', haggling the prices; he shaved, had a meal, and spent two nights at fifteen cents each in Salvation Army beds. One night he went to a theatre; and he walked round the White City, the buildings in Jackson Park of the previous year's World's Fair. Then he set off for St Joseph to call on Flora's sister Mary Everhard, whom he had never seen, and her family.

He was welcomed so warmly that he stayed for some weeks. In letters to her sister, Flora had told of Jack's going to sea and his prowess in winning the writers' competition and having his article published. Jack's aunt took him out and bought him clothes, and gave parties for him; he regaled her with stories of his adventures. She treated him like a hero. He sunbathed, wrote notes in his diary, and explored the countryside. His presence was less gratifying to Mary Everhard's sons. One of them, Harry, wrote later that Jack 'did not make any hit at all with my brother or myself'. Their mother's effusiveness to the visitor, and her insistence that he 'rest' while they did household chores, were obvious reasons for resentment. In addition, Jack privately told them more boastful and less savoury yarns about his doings; they thought him a low-life rather than a champion. Jack's fancy was caught by the name of Harry's brother, Ernest Everhard, and he used it for the hero of *The Iron Heel*.

After leaving the Everhards' home he seems to have travelled from city to city, aiming to see everything he could — riding the rods and the blinds, of course, and throwing his feet for meals and tobacco. He went to Canada, sight-seeing in Montreal and Ottawa; to New York; Boston; Pittsburgh and Baltimore. To some extent he was an observer, sometimes noting down and always remembering whatever he came across. The diary entries reflect this conscious seeking, as when he reflected on the 'hopeless, friendless condition' of tramps he met: 'I always said that I would not marry till 26 or 27, and I still think that holds good. But I will look around me in the meantime and try and profit by the experience, obtained by others through the lottery of marriage.' Elsewhere he wrote down scraps of dialogue and tramps' slang, copied poems and the words of popular songs, made notes on the question 'Which came into the world first, the chicken or the egg?'

He was increasingly taken up with the idea of a law of life. At one point, in a gypsy camp he saw a man flogging his children and his wife. Jack knew he must not protest or interfere — the woman herself would have turned on him. It was the law. A few years later, when he had been to see an execution in San Quentin jail, he defended it in the same terms against Anna Strunsky's reproach:

> ... by living in this community of people you help to support the Law which this community makes, and when you help to support the Law it means that you pay your share of the rope which is bought to hang the man. Quit or stay with it — that's the proposition. I, for one, stay with it. I am neither afraid nor ashamed of it ... By God! the man who is afraid to take the fish off the hook or the guts from the bird he expects to eat is no man at all.[4]

However, his indignation when the law seized him was from a different frame of mind. The experience, taken for granted by most tramps, bit deeply into him and was a turning-point in his life. He had gone from New York to see Niagara Falls. It was the end of June 1894, a few days before the great American railway strike began. Jack was arrested for vagrancy and lined up, handcuffed to fifteen other men, in court next morning. He saw each man sentenced to thirty days without plea or evidence and with only a few words spoken. He remembered the right of every American to proper trial. He began to speak; the judge said 'Shut up!' before repeating 'Thirty days', and Jack was taken to jail with the rest. His head was shaved, and he was put in prisoners' striped clothes.

On the way to jail he shared his tobacco with a man who had been in prison many times. He showed Jack the ropes; when he was appointed a trusty he secured Jack's appointment too. As a 'hall man', taking the prisoners their bread and water, he had access to extra rations and traded them for tobacco. And he saw the things that took place. He talked to men and listened to their stories,

looked on at and took part in scenes of frightful violence. It was all
to be described in *The Road*. The manhandling by the guards;
Jack's own minor job, supervising the morning wash, of hitting
any man who spoke with a broom-handle end-on in the face; the
incident of the young man who was battered down five flights of
steel stairs and ended lying 'wholly naked and streaming blood
from every portion of the surface of his body'.

The trusty friend wanted Jack to become his partner in petty
crime when they were outside, but Jack — though he assented and
talked over plans — was determined never to risk another jail
sentence. He slipped away from the other man when they were
released, ran for the railroad station and boarded a train. He
resumed travelling between the eastern cities, and fell in with
groups of tramps. He came across men from the broken-up
unemployed armies, abandoned by their leaders and making their
disconsolate and hungry way back across America. However, the
hobos he came across in and round cities were of a different type
from either the road-kids or Kelly's followers. A number of them
were educated men who could not or would not fit in with industrial
society; they sat in parks arguing and expounding. Jack met a
tramp in Boston 'with more knowledge and culture under his rags
than falls to the average man who sits in high places'. For two days
this man talked to him about Marx, Kant and Spencer, and told him
the history of the streets and buildings in Boston; then he vanished.
In Baltimore Jack met a group which included Frank Strawn-
Hamilton, the 'genius, tramp, socialist, etc., etc.' who impressed
him tremendously.[5]

Undoubtedly Jack London's socialism was conceived at this
time. It is always put down to what he saw and experienced in his
travels across America — the discovery of the victims of the
capitalist system and the destruction brought about by it. He
himself put it like that, in 'How I Became a Socialist'. He wrote:
'On rods and blind baggages I fought my way from the open West,
where men bucked big and the job hunted the man, to the congested
labour centres of the East, where men were small potatoes and
hunted the job for all they were worth. And on this new *blond-beast*
adventure I found myself looking upon life from a new and
different angle.'

There is too much of the dramatic in this account which his

biographers have accepted. Apart from the sea, Jack knew little of 'the open West'. Most of the time, he had been raised on poverty-stricken small farms and in the poor quarters of Oakland; what he had seen were the roughest parts of the town and the docksides. Only the seamen 'bucked big' — certainly his assertion about the job hunting the man was pure imagination, as his slaving for ten cents an hour makes plain. The background to 'The Apostate' could have been New York or Chicago, but was Oakland and the cannery in which he had worked; and when he left the West men there were 'small potatoes' indeed, reduced and brought to misery by the depression.

The different angle from which he viewed life was a subjective one. Meeting and listening to trade-unionists and socialists drew his attention to the logic and facts of working-class life: the mercilessness of the labour market, the grinding exploitation, the fate of those who were discarded and lacked the strength to keep up. But his conclusion was principally for himself. He stated it in 'How I Became a Socialist', as the oath he swore when he had seen 'the shambles at the bottom of the Social Pit':

> All my days I have worked hard with my body, and according to the number of days I have worked, by just that much am I nearer the bottom of the Pit. I shall climb out of the Pit, but not by the muscles of my body shall I climb out. I shall do no more hard work, and may God strike me dead if I do another day's hard work with my body more than I absolutely have to.

This is intended as the statement of his rejection of individualism; it is in fact a reaffirmation, an avowal to take individualism to a higher plane.

Jack London's socialism did not derive from experience, but was part of the intellectual atmosphere of the time. Continually seeking knowledge and ideas — in his travels he went and read in libraries, picked up second-hand books, and looked for men who could talk — he was bound to meet and be impressed by the socialist movement in the America of the eighteen-nineties. If he had not come into contact with devotees of Marx and Spencer on the road in the east, his aspirations would have led to them in San Francisco. Of course he related what he learned to what he had experienced; but the class struggle he claimed to have found was precisely what he never understood or identified himself with.

His last months on the road were the most adventurous. In Boston he sold an article on tramping to a new magazine, the *Bostonian*, for ten dollars; then his homeward journey began. According to Charmian and Irving Stone he travelled alone save for encounters with other hobos, and pursuing — as described in *The Road* — his fast-moving namesake Skysail Jack. Joan found that he had a fortnight's company from a young man named Smith, who left him near Vancouver to travel south. According to all three he crossed Canada and went home by sea from Vancouver, working as a stoker on the steamship *Umatilla*.

However, another account is found in a little book called *From Coast to Coast with Jack London by A no.I 'the famous tramp' who travelled 500,000 miles for $761*. It was published in 1917, soon after Jack's death. No attention was paid to it, possibly because of the legion of men who claimed to have known him on the road (during his years of fame there were several impersonators who passed worthless cheques and achieved seductions in his name).

The author of *From Coast to Coast* was identified as Leon Ray Livingston, and his narrative has too many points of authenticity to be dismissed. According to him, he met Jack in New York. He had been giving a story of his own hobo life to Godwin, editor of the *Sunday World* magazine section. In exchange, he was given space to advertise for a companion to travel the hard way back to California. When he went the next day to collect the replies he was challenged by a slightly-built young man of about eighteen who had grey eyes and thick brown hair, with a cap on top. The two liked each other at once; they decided to start out the same evening.

They were turned out of one railway station and went to a goods station. A tramp stole their jackets and shoes while they were sleeping; they were drenched by a water-crane. Jack wanted to detour to Boston but, chased by the guards and police, they boarded a train to Cleveland. With several of the incidents described in *The Road*, they made their way westward. In Chicago they met Martin Johnson, later to be with Jack on the *Snark*[6]; they went by Fairfax, Omaha, Laramie, Salt Lake City, Reno, Truckee, New Castle and Sacramento. In Oakland, Livingston went home with Jack and met his family.

It is possible that Jack's journey through Canada, his meeting with Smith and his chase after Skysail Jack belong to earlier in the year, after he left the Everhards', and that the sequence of events was rearranged in the accounts he gave. None of the biographers gives any details of the Canadian journey except that it ended on the *Umatilla*. Though Jack made no mention of such a companion he and Charmian entertained an 'A no.1, the famous tramp' at Glen Ellen several years later. The locations of Livingston's homeward journey are close to those of Jack's outward passage with Kelly's Army. Probably the truth lies somewhere among the different versions — omissions by Jack, over-statement by Livingston, and the incomplete nature of scraps gathered by the three biographers.

Most of Jack's road-kid adventures belong to this final period. *The Road* captures all its recklessness and romance. Entries in Jack's diary record the hardships: 'The days are burning & the nights freezing cold'; 'woke up at 3.30 a.m. half froze to death'; riding the blind baggage in a blizzard so thick that 'one could not see over a rod ahead'. There are begging, thieving and mugging, and risks of all kinds taken for granted. There were brakemen who would dangle a coupling pin under a carriage when a tramp was riding the rods, aiming for it to strike the rails and beat the tramp to death. Leaping for trains at high speed, road-kids were killed or lost their legs if they slipped. The fraternity left their 'monnikers' carved and scrawled on water-tanks — this was the trail that Skysail Jack made for Sailor Jack to follow. One of the strongest impressions from *The Road* is how these contractors-out of industrial life were expendable. They could be thrown off or under trains without concern. Besides the hobos who would say they had known Jack London, there were policemen and brakemen who might have said they tried to kill him.

The criminal aspects of this life and his prison experience remained alive in Jack's mind. In *John Barleycorn* he said that his vow of no more manual labour also included 'no criminality ... That would be almost as disastrous as to be a labourer.' He was determined to be a writer. In five years when he returned to Oakland he had become one, and started his rise to fame. Yet it was several more years before he used the diaries he had kept. *The Road* was not written until the end of 1906, and he discussed with George Brett of the Macmillan Company, his publishers, whether its publication would damage the sales of his other books.

It is worth noting that his seven months on the road were without drinking, other than occasionally. He arrived home at the end of 1894 free from the depression and demoralisation in which alcohol had played a part at other times. He was anxious to study, be educated, become socially acceptable, and start writing. It seemed to him indispensable to go to college. The obstacles had diminished: John London's health was better and he was in regular work, and the family had moved to a less depressing home. They now had a little cottage in Twenty-second Avenue. Flora was enthusiastic for Jack's writing ambition and, with the help of money from Eliza, furnished his bedroom with a table to work at and a student's lamp. Close to his nineteenth birthday, he became a student at the Oakland High School.

4. College and the Klondike

The gap between Jack and the high-school students was the one he had found between himself and the young men at the YMCA, on his return from sea. They were a little younger in years, far remote in living. He saw them as respectable, nice boys and girls with whom he wanted to join in, but nearly everything about him was alien. He wore shabby casual clothes — baggy spring-bottom trousers, the garb of a waterfront rough, and an open-neck blue shirt. He swore, and was addicted to hand-rolled cigarettes and chewing tobacco. He had already lost all his front teeth through decay; the remainder were badly in need of fillings, and he said he found the tobacco-chewing a relief from pain. The state of his teeth was attributed to neglect, but it seems to have been too spectacular — the likelihood is that he was caries-prone. At any rate, his sister Eliza paid for false teeth for him before he went to high school. She also provided him with a bicycle, one of the new low 'safety wheels'.

As with everything else he had done, Jack threw himself assertively into studying. He ignored subjects which he thought irrelevant to his ends (later he regretted that he had not learned a foreign language). As soon as lessons ended he would put on his cap and leave the classroom; one schoolmate recalled his contemptuous attitude towards the others' hurly-burly and their need to be called to order by the teachers. Though he was secretly eager for acceptance, he had no idea of making concessions. Attending the school debating society, he thrust forward not only book-knowledge of which the others were all the more resentful because they had not suspected it, but also the irreligious philosophies and political radicalism he had learned from his hobo acquaintances.

He went home to study and write. As well as school books, he was getting from the public library the works he had heard about, sitting at the little table in his bedroom until the small hours of every morning. He wrote for the school magazine, the *Aegis*, accounts of his experiences on the road and at sea. They earned a degree of admiration for him and at the same time affirmed the breadth of the gap; he was describing a life rough and unrespectable like himself. He was, too, hanging round meetings in the park near the high school, anxious to learn more about socialism. A branch of the Socialist Labour Party had recently been formed in Oakland and was crusading vigorously from platforms in the streets and parks.

His continual visits to the library brought him what he could not find at school: social acceptance. A new librarian, Frederick Irons Bamford, noted his interest as Ina Coolbrith had done. Bamford was a Christian Socialist, too studious a man for class-struggle militancy but full of the cultural teachings of William Morris, Ruskin, Arnold and Carlyle. He directed Jack to fresh books and a different side of socialism, and possibly conveyed to him the vital rôle writers could play in wakening people to the idea of a better life. Going to the library more and more to talk to Bamford and to read in the reference room, Jack struck up a friendship with a young man named Fred Jacobs.

Fred was working in the library. Like Jack, he was studying and aiming to go to university. He had been to high school and evening classes, but now proposed to pay — with the money earned at the library — for a year at the University Academy, the 'cramming joint' for entrance qualifications. Jack was working in his spare time, doing janitor work at the school. The two boys talked eagerly about their common objective, and Fred introduced Jack to friends who likewise were studying: Jim Reed, Bess Maddern, and Ted and Mabel Applegarth. To his astonishment, he found himself invited to take part in their activities, going to concerts and for cycle rides with them, and asked to their homes to meet their families.

The Madderns and the Applegarths inhabited a different world. It was the one Jack had glimpsed through Miss Coolbrith when he was ten, and more recently in Bamford's talk of Morris and Ruskin. There was no question of condescension or snobbery, but there were good taste and refinement, books and pictures. Ted taught Jack chess, and Bess and Mabel tried to teach him to dance. Accomplishments like these, conventions of the social life to which his new friends were brought up, were infinitely desirable to Jack as symbols of everything to which he was aspiring. He strove to learn and imitate. And, almost as soon as he entered her home, he fell in love with Mabel Applegarth.

The Applegarths had come from England. Mabel's father, a mining engineer, was away from home much of the time, and the virtual head of the family was Mrs Applegarth. She sustained what Jack was incapable of recognising as the British petit-bourgeois way of life, including a stringent domination of her two children. She accompanied them on cycle-rides and picnics, led the conversation, and promoted the 'Fin du Siècle' club which was a regular gathering of friends to discuss literature and music.

Mabel Applegarth's name was not given in Charmian's book: she was referred to as 'the Lily' or 'the Lily Maid'. Undoubtedly the object was to avoid giving embarrassment, but the epithet accurately reflects the nature of Jack's feelings for Mabel. He compared her with a pale gold flower on a slender stem. She was delicate and beautiful, with soft fair hair and fragile white hands — all porcelain delicacy, enhanced by the long clothes of the time. She had been trained to perfection in speech and etiquette; she played the piano and sang, could talk about books, art and poetry. Jack was enchanted. Her physical frailty roused him to protective feelings, and favourable comparisons with other girls he had known in other circumstances.

He was in love with an ideal, of course. Breaking away from his existence so far, drawn by a vision of culture and superiority, he found it all embodied in Mabel. One of his letters to her artlessly asked her opinion of the 'style and thought' of a passage he had come across:

> The effect of the sweetly good woman upon man is like the perfume of a flower that grew in his childhood's garden, or a strain of music heard in his youth. He is ashamed of his grosser appetites when he is in her presence. He would not like her to know of his errors and vices. He feels like another man when near her and realises that he has a spiritual nature. Yet as the effect of the strain of music or the perfume of the

flower is necessary, so often her influence ceases when he is absent from her, unless she be the woman who rules his life.

Without doubt, too, he was unable to comprehend women as persons. It remained the case throughout his life. After the break-up of his first marriage and until his death his letters repeatedly asserted 'all women' to be liars and cheats, that he 'noticed' this and that failing in them — the blusterings of a man whose expectations had been disappointed. He wanted of Mabel what he wanted of all those he knew at different stages, whether oyster-pirates or intellectuals: that they should act the parts in his dream, regardless of what happened when he awoke.

While he hankered in the Applegarths' home and applied himself still more intensely to study, Jack also plunged into political activity. He attended the Socialist Labour Party's Sunday evening lectures and outdoor meetings, and got to know some of the members. One, Herman — 'Jim' — Whitaker, managed a co-operative grocery store. As a younger man he had been a physical training instructor in the British army. Jack became a regular caller at the store, first to discuss socialism and then at night-times to practise fencing and boxing with Jim as his tutor. He learned quickly, admiring their scientific nature in contrast with the wild free-for-all of waterfront brawling.

For the moment he held back from joining the party. He had too many irons in the fire. Despite its proselytising the Oakland branch was given to intellectual debate rather than class-struggle militancy. It had some outstanding people — Strawn-Hamilton, who was to be represented in *Martin Eden*, and Austin Lewis — but its atmosphere at this stage was of a 'progressive' group standing in the name of higher reason against injustice. The seminal books of the socialist movement were only gradually appearing. Marx was talked about but scarcely available, and the flood of translations (several of them by Lewis) of European social-democratic works had not yet begun. Discussion centred instead on the nature and achievement of a 'socialist commonwealth'; the most influential book of the period, in circles like this, was Edward Bellamy's *Looking Backward*.

To a large extent this was what Jack wanted. He was learning and being introduced to books, having his wits sharpened by controversy. But it lacked full-bloodedness. In his months on the road he had not only heard more powerful-sounding revolutionary talk, but had been a witness of strikes in eastern America where the conflict between workers and employers was raw. What he had been stimulated by was the idea of a mass movement of the working class, an army of conquest over the existing order. The image of such a movement could not fail to appeal to him, and he related it to what he had gathered from Darwin and Spencer. It was a matter of the natural triumph of the fittest and strongest: the workers would rise like some giant creature from primeval slime to stand all-powerful.

As the end of his first year in high school approached, he resolved to cut through to university by means of the cramming academy. Ordinarily he would have faced two more high-school years; he was nearly twenty, and impatient to realise his ambitions. The academy catered for the well-to-do and charged stiff fees, but Jack was confident that success would enable him to repay whoever lent the money to him. His sister Eliza did so. He enrolled and started there at the beginning of 1896, attacking the studies with all his energy. He planned to cover the necessary work in four months — that is, to finish in one term only. Sitting up at nights, taking in all the instructors could give him, he raced ahead. After five weeks he was called into the principal's office, paid back his money and told to leave.

The reason given was that his progress had been so remarkable as to create resentment among the other students and even to call in question the academy's integrity: more simply, if an assiduous young man could cover the ground in less than a term, what were they paying for? The principal, Mr Anderson, conveyed that Jack's headway had put him in difficulties he could not tolerate; he shook hands, and wished Jack luck. Had he been wholly acceptable, he might have been asked to slow down or mark time for a month or two. As it was, he carried a wild reputation which was confirmed by his appearance and manner and his taking part in socialist meetings in the streets.

He joined the Socialist Labour Party almost immediately after the academy's rejection, in April 1896, and his sense of grievance almost certainly provided the final impetus. Nevertheless, he would not be put off from his determination to go to university. Aware of what the entrance examinations required, and of how far he had already gone towards them, he went on studying in his room at home. He was helped in physics by Fred Jacobs and in mathematics by Bess Maddern. For twelve weeks he toiled over books nineteen hours a day, giving himself little relief. The twitching of his boyhood returned; he was as exhausted as he had been when he shovelled coal for two men.

The examinations, held in the Mechanics' Building at Berkeley, began on 10 August and lasted several days. Something Jack did not know was that the university was in such demand that it raised its entrance qualifications in 1896 without advertising the fact. He sat writing away, all the concentration and work of the preceding months brought to their climax. There was nothing more he could do. As soon as the examinations were finished he felt near-revulsion — 'didn't want to see a book … nor to think nor to lay eyes on anybody who was liable to think'.

Most students waited to learn the results in a few days. He went to the estuary next morning and borrowed a small boat. At the foot of it he put a roll of bedding and some food, and let the wind carry him into Suisun Bay. He intended to cross it and sail into the San Joaquin, and keep sailing until the wind or the tide changed. In the afternoon the sight of Benicia on his port side revived old memories. He altered course, headed for the wharf he knew so well, and tied up there. As he expected, he did not have to look far for acquaintances. They made for Jorgenson's saloon, calling for whiskey.

At some stage during the drinking bout someone moved Jack's small craft and transferred his gear into a bigger, roomier Columbia River salmon boat. Jack left Benicia in it that night, shouting and singing: he poured out addled passages from his studies, chanted problems, bawled sea-shanties and popular songs. He tried to re-create sailing feats from his days with Young Scratch. Then, next day, he cruised on alone. He fished and slept, restoring himself in mind and body, not seeking to drink again. At the end of a week he returned the boat and went home, refreshed.

He had passed the examinations and could enter the university in the autumn. Not only had his first objective been reached; he could now claim equal footing with the friends whose domestic circles he had entered. The university course was for four years, but a diploma was not Jack's intention. He was set on becoming a writer. According to the artist James Hopper, who met and listened to him on the campus:

> He was full of gigantic plans — just as, indeed, I was to find him always whenever I came upon him later in life ... He was going to take all the courses in English, all of them, nothing less. Also, of course, he meant to take most of the courses in the natural sciences, many in history, and bite a respectable chunk out of the philosophies.

Hopper had seen Jack before, as a boy in Alameda. He found him now self-confident, sturdy and immensely attractive: 'a strange combination of Scandinavian sailor and Greek god'. He recalled also his own misgivings. Already in his second year at Berkeley, he was able to see that Jack's expectations of what he would gain from the university were too high. He did not say so, and if he had it would not have been effective.

In the few months he was there, Jack applied himself as intensely as ever. He spent countless hours in the university library, cramming into himself everything which appeared relevant. He mixed little with the other students, though his performance in dashing through the high school studies and entrance examinations was whispered-about respectfully. One other exploit astonished them too. The college had advertised for a steeplejack to paint the flagpole in the middle of the campus. Early one morning Jack climbed it; the students arriving for classes watched him working his way down, painting as he went, while the pole swayed in a strong north wind. They were hardly to know that he had climbed the masts of the *Sophie Sutherland* time and again.

Why he left after only one term is not clear. Joan London attributed it chiefly to disappointment, to finding the teachers hostile to new ideas and the courses shallow; and, particularly, to the discovery put into Martin Eden's mouth — 'I can do the work quicker than they can teach me'. Certainly for the rest of his life he spoke contemptuously of academic learning, and described it in a letter to Joan as 'the wheel of university subservience to the ruling class'. Yet in a letter in 1900, supplying autobiographical information to the Houghton Mifflin Company who were publishing *The Son of the Wolf*, Jack regretted that he had been unable to continue at the university. He wrote: 'Was forced, much against my inclinations, to give this over just prior to the completion of my Freshman Year.' And: 'I am always studying. The aim of the university is simply to prepare one for a whole future life of study. I have been denied this advantage, but am knocking along somehow.'

In fact there is nothing to support the idea of swift disillusion, other than the attitude he took when he had become successful. He received A and B grades for his first term's work, had returned from the Christmas vacation and enrolled for the next term when he resigned. The view given by Irving Stone and Charmian, from his own narrative in *John Barleycorn*, is that lack of money for himself and his family compelled him to give it up. It is true that they were again in a poor plight — John London was a sick man peddling on doorsteps in Alameda. However, if their urgent need was the reason, Jack acted inconsistently in the face of it: he sat in his room writing, continuing to add to the household burden ('I suffered my old father to feed me with the meagre remains of his failing strength').

The truth is that Jack learned at this time that John London was probably not his father. There can be only surmise as to who told him. Possibly the discovery was made by accident — the Londons' home was still only a few miles from San Francisco, where the drama had taken place, and Professor Chaney was remembered by many people. The consequences were bound to be catastrophic. Illegitimacy was a huge personal and social stain, a reason in itself why one could not continue at university. Jack's correspondence with Chaney shows the extent to which he was tortured by the thought. He wanted to know not simply who his father was, but whether his mother was 'a loose women' — even, was she diseased?

This alone seems to have been the reason why he suddenly left college, and his subsequent denigration of universities was the posture taken when he found he had reached his goal without their help. The only person he told of his discovery was Ted Applegarth — when he located Chaney, Jack wanted to write from the Applegarths' address so that the reply was not seen at his own home. He told Ted how intense his distress was; presumably also he asked him not to tell Mabel, for the matter is not referred to in

Jack's letters to her. The effect on his relationship with his mother and stepfather is not marked in any way. In later years he spoke of John London with respect, but was always ready to treat Flora as a misfortune. A letter to Charmian's aunt, Ninetta Eames, in 1907, said : 'There is one thing at least, upon which you and I agree — namely, the character, of my mother ... Let me tell you right now that you have not seen one thousandth part of the real devil that she is.'

Perhaps fortunately, in the week in February 1897 that Jack left the university there was another kind of excitement in his life. The Socialist Labour Party of Oakland was protesting against a city ordnance under which street meetings within the city's fire limits were prohibited. Its decision was to hold a meeting and make a test case; the day for it would be Abraham Lincoln's birthday and the volunteer to be sacrificed was Jack London. Supported by Jim Whitaker, he took the stand — he was a poor extempore speaker, and was thankful when the police arrived to stop the meeting and take him to jail. Nothing ensued: Jack was acquitted, the law was unchanged. Only a little fame was gained. He was interviewed and dubbed 'the boy socialist' by reporters, and Mabel Applegarth disapproved. The incident provided a distraction, however, at a time when he sorely needed it.

Jack described this period in his life in *John Barleycorn*. The three biographers all accepted this account. It begins: 'I decided immediately to embark on my career.' It relates how he tried poetry, stories, essays and comic pieces and struggled with an ancient typewriter which had only capital letters and had to be struck so hard as to be painful; and sent manuscripts to editors everywhere, without success. All this was in the early months of 1897. Yet a letter from him offering an article to a paper called *The Bulletin*, dated 17 September 1898, has written across the top in Charmian's hand: 'This is Jack's first letter to an editor' — though she reproduced the *John Barleycorn* version.

The story does not ring true, in fact. Jack left college on 4 February 1897; he was arrested on the 12th. In July he and Eliza's husband left San Francisco aboard the *Umatilla*, equipped for the Yukon and the gold rush. In between, he worked and lived for a period of months in a steam laundry. His story speaks of manuscripts from his huge output making 'amazing round-trip records between the Pacific and the Atlantic'. There is too much activity to fit in the time which also includes his writing to Chaney and receiving the replies, being in contact with the Applegarths and keeping up his political interest (he wrote to Ted Applegarth in June expressing enthusiasm for the formation of the Social Democracy of America).

One has to conclude that the *John Barleycorn* narrative pulls a curtain over his life at the time. The period of writing and submitting innumerable manuscripts belongs to a little later, after his return from the Yukon. When his university life ended he was, more than anything else, unhappy and uncertain, and took the steam-laundry job without much delay.

The laundry was at Belmont Academy, a military school on the peninsula to the south of San Francisco. It had modern machinery, and Jack and another young man did all the sorting, washing and ironing. The toil was endless, going on late at night for six days a week. He was paid thirty dollars a month and board, eating in the kitchen. 'By Saturday night,' he wrote, 'we were frazzled wrecks.' The experience was related in detail in *Martin Eden*, where he wrote of 'the maggots of intoxication' as the inevitable, insistent relief (though in *John Barleycorn* he claimed not to have drunk while in the laundry). He took a pile of books with him but was too exhausted to read.

When the Academy closed for the summer vacation he went home to Oakland, slept, saw his friends, and looked for another job. Just as Kelly's Army had been creating a stir when he was in the same situation three years before, there was now another and much greater excitement: the gold rush to the Klondike had begun. Though Jack was attracted immediately by the possibility of 'striking it rich', for him as for hundreds of thousands of others there was also the magnetism of a new frontier, going into unknown territory to find adventures and opportunities which had not existed before.

Jack cast about desperately to raise the money for clothing and equipment, food supplies and the journey. He went to see the poet Joaquin Miller, whom he had met at socialist meetings, confident that he would understand and lend the money; but Miller himself had left for the Klondike on a journalistic assignment. He thought he could not ask his sister, who had helped him so often. Yet it was from Eliza's household that the means came, unexpectedly. Her elderly husband James Shepard caught the gold-fever. He mortgaged his home and his shares in a small business, and in order to have youth and experience beside him offered to take Jack as his partner. In fact Shepard was in no shape to go adventuring. Before their preparations had begun he had a heart attack on a streetcar and was ordered to bed to rest. Nevertheless they toured San Francisco buying furs, mining equipment, tents and blankets, materials to build sleds and canoes. Jack's cargo weighed nearly 2000 lb.

He wrote to Mabel telling her he was going. The reply was a near-hysterical one from her mother: 'Oh, dear John, do be persuaded to give up the idea, for we feel certain that you are going to meet your death, and we shall never see you again ... Your Father and Mother must be nearly crazed over it. Now, even at the eleventh hour, dear John, do change your mind and stay.' No appeal would have turned him back, and there were deeper concerns in his home: his stepfather was dying. He and Shepard sailed through the Golden Gate on 25 July. On board they formed a partnership with three other men.

For very many of the venturers, including Shepard, the expedition was over quickly. The gold rush produced a saying: 'Two dollars go into the ground for each dollar that comes out.' When the steamers put down their hordes of passengers and freight, the Coast Range mountains stood before them snow-covered and formidable: this was what they had to cross to start the journey to Dawson City. There were a small number of Indians and pack-horses, plying at scarcity prices — thirty cents to carry every pound. Some turned back at this stage; others dragged their loads to attempt the passes. Jack and his party camped overnight and decided on the Chilkoot pass. At this point Shepard, having heard stories of the hardships and difficulties from returning men, decided he had had enough. To Jack's relief, he left their equipment and waited for the next steamship home. He arrived in Oakland just before John London's death; his wife, John's daughter Eliza, paid for the funeral.

Jack started the ascent of the Chilkoot pass next morning with the other three. He carried more than his share and toiled to keep ahead. After they reached the top, they made their way down to the chain of glacial lakes which would take them into the Lewes River and thence to the Yukon.He quickly formulated an ideal of supremacy, as he had among oyster-pirates and tramps: he would outdo the best on the trail — in this case, the Indians themselves. He wrote later: 'I remember at the end of the twenty-eight mile portage across Chilkoot from Dyea Beach to Lake Linderman, I was packing up with the Indians and outpacking many an Indian. The last pack into Linderman was three miles. I back-tripped it four times a day, and on each forward trip carried one hundred and fifty pounds. This means that over the worst trails I daily traveled twenty-four miles, twelve of which were under a burden of one hundred and fifty pounds.'

At Linderman they bought boards cut from fresh-felled trees and made a boat. One of Jack's companions, Merritt Sloper, was a boat-builder. Jack cut, stitched and rigged a sail; they were saved continual rowing, and the *Yukon Belle* was so soundly constructed that their supplies remained dry even in the rapids. Now they drove on, with the freeze-up at their heels. They slept as little as possible. At Lake Marsh the North-west Mounted Police stopped any man going on unless he had seven hundred pounds of food. At Lake Lebarge a driving blizzard held them up for three days; then, at Jack's insistence, they forced their way on or they would have had to camp there for the winter. They fought their way across yard by yard, watching the lake freeze behind them.

The most violent and dangerous episodes on the trip were shooting Box Canyon and White Horse Rapids. In each of these, Jack elected to run through because of the time it would take — perhaps two days — to pull the boat over land and carry its loads. Undoubtedly his sailing skill and the nerve found in his exploits with Young Scratch Nelson took them through. In Box Canyon the water is thrown back from high rock walls to make a great whirling crest in the centre. Struggling with the oars — Sloper's broke — they rode the waves and were flung through the whirlpool. Then there were two miles of ordinary rapids before they reached the White Horse, where for years everyone who tried had been drowned. With a thousand people watching and the wrecks of other boats lying on the rocks, they shot triumphantly through the hostile waters. Asked to take other boats through, Jack charged twenty-five dollars each; he and his group stayed several days, and collected three thousand dollars.

On 9 October they reached Upper Island, off the eastern bank of the Yukon, eighty miles from Dawson. Here Jack and his companions stopped in a log cabin, one of several abandoned by the Bering Sea fur traders; that the cabins were empty is a mark of how far ahead they had forged. Three days later they went to Henderson Creek to stake their claims, then down to Dawson to register them. They stayed in Dawson, the Yukon's metropolis, for nearly two months. Returning to Upper Island, they waited for spring to come and prospecting to begin. But there was to be no gold for Jack. Like others, he was attacked by scurvy — they could get no fresh vegetables. He had learned in a letter that John London was dead. Sick and penniless, he left Dawson for home in June of 1898.

In his gold-rush year Jack found scenes, happenings and characters for some of his most outstanding stories. He met Elam Harnish, called 'Burning Daylight', and took both names and much of the man's character for one of his heroes; he observed the dogs on which *The Call of the Wild* was to be founded; the Malemute Kid; the exploits, if not the person, of Smoke Bellew. However, the months in the little colony at Upper Island provided other material of almost equal importance. The mining camps, like the lumber camps, had a great deal of political consciousness. In the sixty or so men on Upper Island were several from universities and the professions. Their centre was Louis Savard's cabin, and there they sat in front of log fires talking and arguing all day over philosophy, economics, and the new scientific doctrines.

Jack had taken a pile of books with him. One of the party, W.B.Hargrave, recalled his enthusiasm and mental agility in the endless discussions. There is a story of an old prospector, caught in a storm and half-dead, stumbling into the cabin one night and finding a crowd of men in ferocious dispute; when he understood that they were discussing socialism, he thought he had gone mad. What Hargrave also noted was a curious lack of discrimination in Jack's reading and judgements. He thought Harrison Ainsworth a master of literature, and revered and quoted some doggerel poetry which appeared in the Klondike newspaper. Hargrave thought the reverence was for print itself: whatever had achieved publication was to be admired.

In this atmosphere, Jack's range of thought widened; his belief in socialism was fed and strengthened; and his determination to become a writer grew. The excitement of the gold-rush faded away. In 1900, in an article on 'The Economics of the Klondike', he wrote:

> The new Klondike, the Klondike of the future, will present remarkable contrasts with the Klondike of the past. Natural obstacles will be cleared away or surmounted, primitive methods abandoned, and the hardship of toil and travel reduced to the smallest possible minimum. Exploration and transportation will be systematised. There will be no waste energy, no harum-scarum carrying on of industry. The frontiersman will yield to the laborer, the prospector to the mining engineer, the dog-driver to the engine-driver, the trader and speculator to the steady-going modern man of business; for these are the men in whose hands the destiny of the Klondike will be intrusted.

The scurvy covered him with sores and weakened his remaining teeth. After a short spell in the Catholic hospital he made his way down the Yukon in a small open boat with two other men. They floated fifteen hundred miles to the Bering Sea, camping on shore at nights. Jack kept a diary again during the journey, noting particularly what he saw in the Indian camps they passed. At St Michael's he took a job stoking on a boat to British Columbia, went to Seattle, and then made his way to Oakland on freight trains. Perhaps the beginning and end of his Klondike journey were transferred to the story of the road — the *Umatilla*, and working as a stoker again on his way home. He arrived with little to look forward to; yet he was about to start his swift rise to fame.

5. Ambitions Realised

On his return Jack looked for work. His mind seems to have been divided between the strong desire to write and the feeling that he must support his widowed mother. Flora was behind with the rent and there were unpaid bills; Eliza, who helped out, was away on a camping holiday. For some time too there had been an additional mouth to feed. Johnny Miller, a grandson of John London's first marriage, had come to be minded while his mother was at work and had become practically a foster-child.

It was impossible to find work. Jack pawned his bicycle, a silver watch Shepard had given him for the Klondike trip, and the raincoat John London had left. He applied for jobs in laundries and factories, and answered an advertisement for a studio model. In August, when he had been home a month, he joined briefly a local rush for gold in the California mountains. He went back to the odd jobs of his boyhood, cleaning windows and cutting lawns and hedges. At the same time he wrote stories about the Klondike and sent them to newspapers and magazines. The first was not even acknowledged; another brought an editorial note saying 'Interest in Alaska has subsided in an amazing degree.' He produced a 20,000-word serial in seven days and sent it, unsuccessfully again, to *The Youth's Companion*.

During the summer he applied for a postman's job; he took the entrance examination, then had to wait for the outcome. His prowess when previously he had set his mind to examinations may have led to its being taken for granted that he would pass, and the idea of his having such a job was favoured by his family and friends. Flora encouraged him to stay at home — she was receiving a small pension and had started giving piano lessons again. Eliza, too, was anxious for Jack to find steady respectable employment.

She had always believed in him, admired his ability, and continually helped him. In a letter that year to Mabel Applegarth he wrote about her, probably aptly:

> If I had followed what she would have advised, had I sought her I would today be a clerk at forty dollars a month, a railroad man, or something similar. I would have winter clothes, go to the theatre, have a nice circle of acquaintances, belong to some horrible little society like the WRC, talk as they talk, think as they do, do as they do ... because I showed that my brain was a little better than it should have been, considering my disadvantages, and lack of advantages; because I was different from most fellows in my station; because of all this she took a liking to me. But all this was secondary; primarily, she was lonely, had no children, a husband who was no husband, etc., she wanted someone to love.

The wishes for his future that he attributed to Eliza were Mabel's own. She was still his girl-friend, but his idealistic worship of her had gone. The year's absence in the Klondike had had its own effect, and he was subjected now to insistent gentle remonstrations which were not far removed from nagging. Mabel was distressed by his shabbiness and palpable lack of food and sleep, and, most of all, by his failure to make a living. She urged him towards the postman's job or any other which would provide stability. She had indeed a strong affection for him and wanted to marry him; she could not understand the harshness with which he replied to her. Her physical weakness also played a part. In one way it still fulfilled Jack's idea of the male giving strength and protectiveness. But his instincts drew him to a sturdier, earthier type of girl of whom the Queen of the Oyster Pirates was the prototype — 'some great wanton flame of a woman', as Brissenden says in *Martin Eden*. In this frame of mind Mabel's frailty and gentility were irritations. He noticed other women; he was even aware of being roused by Mrs Applegarth's vivaciousness.

He still sought Mabel in the belief that her culture and literary knowledge were superior to his. He sent his writings to her for criticism and then was exasperated because she missed the point; and his persistence only made her beg him to give up this ridiculous dream. At the beginning of the 'duty' letter he wrote: 'I do appreciate your interest in my affairs, but — we have no common ground. In a general, vaguely general, way, you know my aspirations; but of the real Jack, his thoughts, feelings, etc., you are positively ignorant.'[7]

Despair bit deeply into him again and again. He spoke about suicide to Mabel and to a boyhood friend, Frank Atherton. Writing to Mabel in November 1898 he said: 'I do not know when I can be down — I may be digging sewers or shovelling coal next week.' Eliza gave him money to buy writing paper and tobacco; when he went to the Applegarths' home for a meal he had difficulty in restraining his hunger. Nor were there other friends in his daily life to whom he could turn for support. He still went to socialist meetings and visited Whitaker for boxing bouts. Strawn-Hamilton applauded his desire to write. The group of friends to whose houses Jack had gone in his college days had dispersed, however. Fred Jacobs had enlisted in the Spanish-American war and was to die of fever. His sweetheart, Bess Maddern, was still in Oakland studying, and Jack occasionally saw her, but only as a link with other times.

He was still awaiting the result of his examination. On 7 January 1899, in a letter, he wrote: 'In the midst of *Youth's Companion* MS., broke off to take Civil Service Examinations for the Post Office. They are very slow at Washington, however, for I have yet to receive my standing in the same. I think I did very well.' In the meantime he went on writing. He had no thought of creating masterpieces. He wanted commercial success — to find the way to make money from writing. He had read in a Sunday newspaper that the minimum rate paid by magazines was ten dollars a thousand words; the arithmetic of it stimulated Jack to seek ways to reap this harvest. He pored over magazines in the public library, trying to discover their technique. He wrote lists of words and hung them round his room, replacing them with more when the words were thoroughly mastered. He worshipped Kipling: he copied out whole stories by Kipling to try to absorb the style and make it his own.

At the beginning of December the first acceptance came, a day or two after he had written his long, bitter letter to Mabel. It was from the *Overland Monthly*, which Bret Harte had founded. They thought so highly of his story 'To the Man on the Trail' that, despite a mass of material on hand, they proposed to publish it at once — in the January issue: 'If you can content yourself with five dollars.' It was almost as great a disillusionment to Jack as all the rejections had been. The story had between three and four thousand words in it, and had taken five days to write; he was being offered the same pay as in the cannery and the jute mill — a dollar a day. He wrote angrily to Mabel: 'if worthy of publication, it were worthy of proper pay'. What he did not realise was that the *Overland Monthly* had high prestige but no money; its acceptance of his story, disappointing as the terms were, was to be invaluable to him.

He wrote to *The Youth's Companion* asking about the serial he had sent. The editor's reply was a rejection; it said that chapters must not exceed 3,500 words, and urged Jack to give up thinking of writing for a living. Jack counted the words and found they were within the limit set. His letter pointing this out also indicates what must have given rise to the editor's advice; it apologised for the first letter, said he had been sick and confused, with 'no friend to go to and had to break out on somebody'. To the editor this unknown young man must have appeared half-demented, and would be better advised to find an undemanding quiet job. Yet, when demoralisation seemed about to overcome him, the miraculous happened: another acceptance. This time the magazine was *The Black Cat*, whose editor, H.D.Umbstaetter, had done much to encourage young writers.

The manuscript Jack had sent was a horror story called 'By a Thousand Deaths'. Umbstaetter asked about its originality, said he found it too wordy, and offered forty dollars if Jack would agree to it being cut to half its length. It was 4,000 words; with the reduction to 2,000 made, he was to receive pay at the rate of twenty dollars a thousand words. This as much as the acceptance itself restored Jack's mind and emotions. He was not chasing wild geese after all; his estimate of what could be made by writing had been more than correct. He wrote to Umbstaetter immediately, and received his payment almost by return. He took the bicycle, watch and raincoat out of pawn, bought food, paid the rent, and equipped himself with stationery. Some years later, in the introduction to a selection of his *Black Cat* stories, he wrote: 'I was at the end of my tether, beaten out, starved, ready to go back to coal shoveling or ahead to suicide … Literally, and literarily, I was saved by the *Black Cat* short story.' Perhaps he was advertising for Umbstaetter and being a little too vociferous. Nevertheless, there is no doubt that this was his turning point.

The *Overland Monthly* accepted another story, 'The White Silence', for February and the editor, James Howard Bridge, asked Jack to go and see him. He explained fully the magazine's financial position, but also emphasised the prestige it still had. He wanted Jack to contract to write six stories. He would be paid only seven-and-a-half dollars each, but they would establish a reputation for him as other magazines might not, and ensure the attention of reviewers and serious readers. In the last week of January he learned the result of his examination. He had passed it with 85.38 per cent and was first on the list for a vacancy. He would start at forty-five dollars a month, rising to sixty-five; but he might have to wait a year for the vacancy. It did not matter now. He was in print.

Financially he was still struggling. He wrote to Mabel at the end of February: 'You know how we are living from hand to mouth, nothing coming in except what is earned, and much of my stuff is in pawn and bills running galore.' He produced hack work — poems, jokes, anything to obtain publication. The *Overland* failed to produce payment, and Jack rowed across the bay to invade its office and threaten violence. He got five dollars from the pockets of the assistant editors, Roscoe Eames and Edward Payne.[8] In the spring he and Flora were down to a few cents and scraps of food. But he was full of confidence and assertiveness now. They are shown in the letters to Cloudesley Johns that began in February 1899. Johns, a post-office employee who was also an aspiring writer and a socialist, was impressed by Jack's first two stories in the *Overland Monthly* and wrote to him. They corresponded prolifically in the next three years, and remained friends throughout Jack's life. In his second letter to Johns, Jack is criticising a manuscript the other man had sent him in editorial tones: advising cuts, to keep off this and that and to watch his vocabulary.

The correspondence reveals a great deal. Jack adopted a special manner for Johns as he did for each person in letters; this was a punchy, lively, man-to-man approach. The second letter ends with a physical description of himself, Johns having asked for a photograph:

23 years of age last January. Stand five feet seven or eight in stocking feet — sailor life shortened me. At present time weigh 168 lbs; but readily jump same pretty close to 180 when I take up outdoor life and go to roughing it. Am clean shaven — when I let 'em come, blonde moustache and black whiskers — but they don't come long. Clean face makes my age enigmatical, and equally competent judges variously estimate my age from twenty to thirty. Greenish-grey eyes, heavy brows which meet; brown hair ... Face bronzed through many long-continued liaisons with the sun, though just now, owing to bleaching process of sedentary life, it is positively yellow. Several scars — hiatus of eight front upper teeth, usually disguised with false plate. There I am in toto.

He did not mention his poverty to Johns. On the contrary, he spoke of the host of friends and old shipmates who were always dropping in, and his inability to refuse when they touched him for loans (this was written at the end of March 1899, at the time when he and Flora were almost starving); and the way in which women friends came to him to have their troubles straightened out. He professed himself a philanderer: 'As passionate as you, with probably less curb, I think I must have been created for some polygamous country. While I have a strong will, I deliberately withhold it when it happens to clash with desire.' He spoke about how he liked to be dressed — 'I like the clean feeling of well fitting clothes, etc.'

It was not a pose, but a vision of himself as he intended to be very soon. One other personal element presents itself in the Johns correspondence. Two months after it began Jack wrote: 'All my life I have sought an ideal chum — such things as ideals are never attainable anyway. I never found the man in whom the elements were so mixed that he could satisfy, or come anywhere near satisfying my ideal ... From what I have learned of you, you approach as nearly as any I have met. But, personality, as reflected by pen and paper, and personality face to face, are two very different things. But I imagine you to have the two main things I have sought.' He carried this desire for a close relationship with an intellectually and physically gifted male — the great 'Man-Comrade' — into his friendship with George Sterling a few years later, and it is impossible not to notice the homosexual overtones in what Joan London called 'the emotional interplay' between them.

But, more than anything else, Cloudesley Johns and Jack talked about achieving success as writers. How many words a day should be aimed at? How much did this or that magazine pay? How were poems and comic stories placed? They exchanged their experiences with editors, discussed vocabulary and phrasing, sent cuttings, and recommended to each other books to read. An article of Jack's called 'On the Writer's Philosophy of Life' was published in 1903 and therefore read as the advice of an established author; however, it was written and first submitted in 1899, and was distilled largely from his correspondence with Johns. The correspondence yields a clear view of the professionalism of Jack's approach. In 1900, when *McClure's* had just paid him three hundred dollars for two stories and an article, he wrote:

> Best pay I have yet received. Why certes, if they wish to buy me body and soul, they are welcome — if they pay the price. I am writing for money; if I can procure fame, that means more money. More money means more life to me. I shall always hate the task of getting money; every time I write it is with great disgust. I'd sooner be out in the open wandering around most any old place.

The passage ends, presciently: 'So the habit of money-getting will never become one of my vices. But the habit of money spending, ah God! I shall always be its victim.'

This statement of personal materialism may sound as if he were striking an attitude; but he was not. In a letter to Anna Strunsky he half-derided Johns for seeking to write 'for posterity', and ended: 'What wouldn't I give just to be able to sit down and write ambitious work? But then it doesn't pay, and I don't.'[9] These declarations of intention made at the outset of his career deserve notice. Jack London was criticised by his well-wishing contemporaries, and the point has often been made since, for falling short of his highest capabilities as a writer: in effect, for writing for the market. In fact he did not conceal from the beginning that this was his purpose, and all his preparation was for it.

In May, June and July more of his stories — most of them about Alaska — were published in a widening range of newspapers and magazines. Happy and elated, Jack took Mabel for a cycle ride. In the hills he sat and told her of his triumphs and his hopes for the future. She asked how much he was getting for the stories, and then wept. To her it was not triumph, but confirmation of what she believed: that he would be far better off as a postman. He admitted that a vacancy had been offered and he had refused it. Still trying to convince her, Jack read to her a manuscript he had brought with him, a new story he was submitting to the editors. Mabel was not placated. The story, like most of the others, was crude and violent; it was hopeless to think of living by writing such things for paltry sums. Why would he not give it up?

This was virtually the end of the romance. In one way it is sad. Though Mabel and Jack were eminently unsuited to each other, she knew him when he was bitterest and most despondent. He never forgave her for her lack of belief in him. The story was dramatised in *Martin Eden*; her family were shown as self-righteous and petty and she — as Ruth — a weak, pathetic creature. However, by this time he did not need moral support. He knew he was on his way to success, and there were others to say it as well since the appearance of his stories in the *Overland Monthly*. The Oakland newspapers which had called him 'the boy socialist' were writing of him respectfully as 'Mr Jack London, the boy author'. Flora was no longer the resigned victim of his waywardness, but zealous to encourage it. Though they did not talk much to each other, she was determined for Jack to succeed and accepted the hardships valiantly. Perhaps for her it meant a rehabilitation: her son's achievement would bring not only comfort and status, but justify what had happened in San Francisco twenty-four years before.

Jack aimed at the new magazines. William Randolph Hearst had not yet arrived on the scene, but in the 'eighties modern journalism was set on its feet by *Munsey's*, *McClure's*, and J.B.Walker's *Cosmopolitan*. Their founders may be seen as men of vision and acumen. What lay behind them were the rapid growth of a vast new reading public and technical innovations which made cheap publication possible — while the great hurly-burly of American life awaited its expression in print. These magazines sold for ten cents a copy, filling a field which the older ones — *Harper's, Scribner's, Atlantic Monthly* — had never envisaged at twenty-five cents and over. In July the *Cosmopolitan* announced a two-hundred dollar prize competition for the best article on 'Loss by lack of Co-operation'. Jack entered it and won.

His essay was called 'What Communities Lose by the Competitive System'. He put into it what he had learned at socialist meetings, in the discussions in Louis Savard's cabin, and from his reading. He thought it would be too radical for the *Cosmopolitan*, though he was pleased with his work in it. When he heard that it was the prizewinner he wrote to Johns: 'I flatter myself that I am one of the rare socialists who have ever succeeded in making money out of their socialism.' In fact it was hardly a revolutionary piece, particularly compared with the élan of his subsequent writings on socialism. He argued rationally that competition bred waste and inefficiency, and needed to be replaced by a planned society.

But before this he had an acceptance from the *Atlantic Monthly*. They bought his long short story 'An Odyssey of the North' for a hundred and twenty dollars. It came in July, 1899 — just twelve months after he returned to Oakland from the Klondike. The *Atlantic*'s standing as a literary magazine was so high that publication in it constituted recognition. Jack may have felt overwhelmed; at any rate he wrote of it to Johns in a matter-of-fact manner that must have been feigned. Another magazine, the *Arena*, had accepted the first of his pieces about the road. 'Think I'll resurrect some of my old retired third rate work and send it to *Harper's, Century*, etc.,' he wrote. 'That is, if there is any chance of their accepting what tenth class publications have refused.'

After the *Atlantic* acceptance he put together a collection of stories and sent it to Houghton Mifflin and Co. of Boston. It was accepted for publication in the spring of 1900, under the title *The Son of the Wolf*.[10] The reader's report on it shows why Jack's stories were finding favour:

> He uses the current slang of the mining camps a little too freely, but his style has freshness, vigor and strength. He draws a vivid picture of the terrors of cold, darkness and starvation, the pleasures of human companionship in adverse circumstances, and the sterling qualities which the rough battle with nature brings out. The reader is convinced that the author has lived the life himself.

At the end of the year the San Francisco section of the Socialist

Labour Party asked him to lecture for it. His talk, in the Union Square Hall, was advertised by posters and handbills announcing him as Jack London 'The Distinguished Magazine Writer'.

On the day *The Son of the Wolf* was published, 7 April 1900, he married Bess Maddern. None of his biographers has been able to say much of what led up to the marriage. Wanting more space, Jack had found a larger house for Flora and himself. According to Charmian, Bess came to help Jack's sister Eliza to fit it out; his decision that he would marry her was made on the spur of the moment, watching her at work in his new home. Joan's version — and it must not be forgotten that she was their daughter — is that companionship between them grew and deepened over a period. They studied English together, went for cycle rides, took photographs and developed them at night. Joan acknowledged the suddenness of the decision; Jack was still speaking of having 'never been rash enough' to take a wife only two weeks before it happened.

Certainly his friends were taken by surprise. To Cloudesley Johns he wrote at the end of a letter on 3 April: 'You must be amused, lest you die. Here goes. You will observe that I have moved. Good. Next Saturday I shall be married. Better? Eh?' Johns's letter in reply consisted simply of: 'Jesus H. Christ!' The same day, Jack wrote to Mrs Ninetta Eames, wife of the business manager of the *Overland Monthly*:

> You know I do things quickly. Sunday morning, last, I had not the slightest intention of doing what I am going to do. I came down and looked over the house I was to move into — that fathered the thought. I made up my mind. Sunday evening I opened transactions for a wife; by Monday evening had the affair well under way; and next Saturday morning I shall marry — a Bessie Maddern, cousin to Minnie Maddern Fiske.[11] ... I shall be steadied, and can be able to devote more time to my work. One only has one life, after all, and why not live it? Besides, my heart is large, and I shall be a cleaner, wholesomer man because of a restraint being laid upon me instead of being free to drift wheresoever I listed. I am sure you will understand.

The letter ended: 'Wedding is to be private.' Charmian, who

was Mrs Eames's niece, attributed to her aunt the immediate judgement that Jack was mistaken in going in for 'a *sensible, considered marriage*'. It was nothing of the kind, of course. It was an impulsive idea, accompanied by reservations and resolutions as naive as his talk of being made 'a cleaner, wholesomer man' by restraint. Fred Jacobs, whom Bess had been going to marry, had died only a short time previously (his body was brought home for a funeral in Oakland in February). Bess must have made clear that she could not so swiftly adapt her emotions, and Jack in turn declared that passion was not what he sought. In a letter to her in 1911 he said: 'Remember, that when I asked you to marry me, and you accepted me, that it was there and then stated explicitly by me that I did not love you. You accepted me on that basis.'

His earlier letter to Johns gives the key. He was impatient to be seen living the life he had depicted — surrounded by friends of both sexes, hospitable and open-handed, wearing the clothes he liked. He had expressed, too, a strong desire to have children. The move to 1130 East 15th Street provided the scenery, as it were. It was a two-storey house with seven rooms and a neat little garden. One room was to be his study, where he had already had shelves made for books; another was a large bay-windowed parlour where he would entertain his friends. All that was lacking was someone to act as hostess, give true domestic charm to the home, and bear children for him. He seems to have nominated Bess for these requirements much as an employee would be chosen at an interview, and asked to start at once.

Poor Bess! In her frame of mind after losing Fred, an offer in such terms was apparently acceptable. Moreover, if Jack had been capable of restrained domesticity the marriage might have had a chance. Presumably Bess shared the anticipations which her fiancé had described to Jack in the past:

> ... a picture such as Fred used to draw is before me. A comfortable little cottage, a couple of servants, a select coterie of friends, and above all, a neat little wife and a couple of diminutive models of us twain ... a cosy grate fire, the sleepy children cuddling on the floor ready for bed, a sort of dreamy communion between the fire, my wife and myself; an assured, though quiet and monotonous, future in prospect; a satisfied knowledge of the many little amenities of civilised

life which are mine and shall be mine. (Letter to Mabel Applegarth, Christmas 1898).

What Jack omitted from the attempted realisation of his vision of himself was the propensity he mentioned to Johns. His desires were strong, and he did not contemplate denying them: 'I like' was to be his continual phrase, the justification for everything. Possibly he thought that marriage to Bess would somehow keep his emotions in order, that monogamy had its own mechanism which operated without the need for tending; the artless phrase about being made 'a cleaner, wholesome man' suggests it. Nor was Bess a passionate woman. When he wrote to her in 1911 — it was a furious, accusatory letter about money matters — he said: 'You are suffering from what you deem a sex-offence. You blame me for that sex-offence, never deeming for a moment that it is due to your own sexual shortcoming.'

The truly mysterious factor surrounding the marriage was Jack's relationship with Anna Strunsky. They were introduced in the autumn of 1899, at one of Austin Lewis's lectures. Anna was a seventeen-year-old Russian Jewess of great beauty and rich intellect. She was at Stanford University; her family's home in San Francisco was a centre of warmth and culture. Describing her first meeting with Jack, she wrote: 'I had a feeling of wonderful happiness. To me it was as if I were meeting in their youth, Lassalle, Karl Marx or Byron.' By the end of the year they were corresponding regularly. Anna belonged to the Socialist Labour Party and ardently pursued social and personal ideals — in later years it was thought that her charm had, by bringing affection constantly to her, prevented her abilities from developing. At this stage, before as well as after his marriage, Jack plainly was in love with her and she with him.

It is true that Anna described their friendship as 'tempestuous' and 'a struggle', but its framework was recognised: 'These differences — what were they but the healthy expression of our immaturity, of our aspirations toward the absolute of truth and right and justice, the normal expression, perhaps, of the man and woman equation in the abstract questions concerning life?' As time went by she developed, as others did, more serious and fundamental criticisms of Jack's attitudes. But the question is not of her sentiments but of his. His letters to her were written in a dewy, caressing language; some began 'Dear, dear You', others were interspersed with sighs — 'Ah!' They debated the nature of love in *The Kempton-Wace Letters*. When he parted from Bess it was Anna who was blamed.

He never revealed the truth of the matter to Charmian. She surmised that Anna was implicated in his decision to marry Bess, and suggested that he turned deliberately to someone who was intellectually undemanding — 'his plans for the future were so nicely ordered toward a systematic schedule of writing.' It is hard to imagine Jack's making that kind of sacrifice. If a guess has to be made, it is that Anna refused him; perhaps on the ground that she was too young and would not consider marrying for some years, in any case in a manner that put nothing in the way of their friendship going on. That there had been some check is conveyed in his letter to her in July 1900. It began: 'Comrades!' and went on:

> The ship, new-launched, rushes to the sea; the sliding-ways rebel in weakling creaks and groans; but sea and ship hear them not; so with us when we rushed into each other's lives — we, the real we, were undisturbed. Comrades! Ay, world without end!

6. A View of the Abyss

The Son of the Wolf was an immediate success. Jack London was compared favourably with Kipling and described as 'a natural born story teller'. The *Atlantic Monthly* said: 'The book produces in the reader a deeper faith in the manly virtues of our race.' Its sales were good, though not spectacular, and the critics' acclaim made for ready acceptances by magazines.

At the end of May *McClure's* bought two stories from Jack. He was contributing to the San Francisco *Examiner* and other magazines, working as hard as ever and still exchanging tips with Johns; but the book had whetted his appetite for more ambitious projects. He wrote to *McClure's* outlining the idea of a novel for them to serialise and asking, if they were in favour, whether they would finance him with advances while he wrote it. McClure agreed, and paid Jack a hundred and twenty-five dollars a month while he worked on *A Daughter of the Snows*.

The original agreement was for five months, but he took longer for various reasons. One was the commencement of *The Kempton-Wace Letters* with Anna, involving not only reading her part and writing his own, but seeing and writing to her frequently. Demands for him to speak and write for the socialists were increasing. But the novel itself was troublesome. Almost as soon as he had begun he expressed misgivings. In December the *Cosmopolitan*, following the interest roused by the publication of his essay on competition, wrote offering him a yearly salary to work exclusively for it. Jack refused, but first wrote to *McClure's* asking for confirmation that their payments would continue.

Early in 1901, when *A Daughter of the Snows* was nearly finished, he wrote to Johns: 'Well, I am on the final stretch of the novel, and it is a failure. This is not said in a fit of the blues, but from calm conviction.' And again: 'Shall have the novel done in ten days, now — N.G. [No good] But I know I shall be able to do a good one yet.' His forebodings were right. McClure was extremely disappointed by it. He had accepted and published a collection of Klondike stories to keep Jack's name before the public, but he found insufficient merit in *A Daughter of the Snows* and rejected it. In the summer he terminated the monthly payments and turned down other stories which Jack submitted. Jack had to turn back to the magazines and papers which paid only ten or twenty dollars for articles and stories.

McClure suspected that Jack had written himself out. He had, indeed, done too much in too short a time, both physically and from the point of view of the material he drew upon; he himself was heartily fed up with Alaska. Yet underlying this problem was a greater one which was to be with him all his life. Money, and plans and promises for spending it, ran through his hands and mind faster than he received it. He grew sick of writing. He disciplined himself to write fifteen hundred words a day, but seldom with enjoyment. He was supporting several people and helping several more. In January 1901, by his own account, he was paying thirty dollars a month to Flora and had just provided another thirty-six for neglected bills; he had paid Mammy Jenny's mortgage interest and tax arrears; gave money to a disabled friend; and was contributing to the upkeep of Jim Whitaker, who had a large family and was trying his luck as a writer.[12]

This was besides maintaining himself and Bess, shortly before her first confinement. He did not resent providing for all and sundry; on the contrary, it was part of his picture of himself. He accepted obligations and accumulated debts easily, almost boastfully, looking only for ways to create bigger rewards from writing. Flora, with Johnny Miller and his mother, were installed in a cottage of their own, and Jack and Bess moved three times in less than two years, each time to a larger and more fashionable house. They entertained friends — their 'Wednesday nights' were lavish, crowded evenings which always culminated in Jack reading aloud from his manuscripts. He was a central figure in the Ruskin Club, an intellectual group formed by Frederick Bamford; it met monthly for a dinner followed by a lecture from some radical celebrity.

The birth of their child, though he professed himself

delighted, was an almost catastrophic disappointment to Jack.[13] He had wanted a boy, so intensely as to make himself certain that it would be so. Nine days before, he wrote to Anna: 'And, O Anna, it must be make or break. No whining, puny breed. It must be great and strong. Or — the penalty must be paid. By it, or by me; one or the other.' The baby was a girl. She was destined to become an outstanding woman, but her advent now struck deep into Jack's proud dreams: what would he not have done with a sturdy male child that was his! His self-confidence suffered other blows. After McClure rebuffed him, while he wrote articles and reported events for the San Francisco *Examiner*, a journalist styling himself 'Yorick' gibed at him and called his style an exemplar of yellow journalism. A friend to whom he had been generous cut him ostentatiously in front of his 'crowd'.

A fresh start came at the end of 1901. The Macmillan Company wrote to him offering to publish his work, and asking what he had available. He had been working intermittently at *The Children of the Frost*, a series of Indian stories based on the notes he had made while returning from the Klondike. He offered the collection, when it was finished, to them — at the same time asking if they would advance money to him. The contract was signed, beginning Jack's long association with Macmillan's. They published nearly all the books he wrote in the rest of his life; the duration of the relationship rested chiefly on the understanding of Jack shown by George Brett, the president of the Macmillan Company.

He does not seem to have been elated by this break. Perhaps it represented only a more lucrative outlet for tales of the frozen north; perhaps his failures had made him cautious. McClure had not returned the *Daughter of the Snows* manuscript, since he had in effect purchased it; in 1902 he sold it to J.B.Lippincott, deducted what he had advanced, and paid Jack a balance of $165. It was published in October 1902, at the same time as *The Children of the Frost* and a boys' novel Jack had sold to the Century Company. He was still working at *The Kempton-Wace Letters* with Anna, and invited her to stay in his home to try to cover more ground. She did, but left after a few days, finding Bess hostile. Jack wrote to Cloudesley Johns: 'I shall be impelled to strong drink if something exciting doesn't happen along pretty soon.'

On 21 July he received a telegram from the American Press Association, asking if he would go to South Africa. The Boer War had just ended, and the idea was for Jack to write articles on post-war conditions there. He wired his acceptance and left the next day. Only ten days earlier he had reiterated his pessimism, saying: 'Between you and me, I wish I had never opened the books. That's where I was a fool'. Now he was on his way across America in a train, no doubt recalling previous journeys on the rods and blind baggages. He stopped in New York to see Brett and discuss plans for future publications. At some stage in their talk Jack raised the possibility of breaking his journey in England. He would like to see the London slums and find material in them for fresh writing.

Brett was enthusiastic and pressed him to do it. Jack was to live in the East End, become again a tramp or an unemployed worker, see social conditions from the inside and gather facts. He remained in New York until 30 July, and then left on the *Majestic*. He was already thinking in his rôle as a partisan social observer. To Anna he wrote:

> A week from to-day I shall be in London. I shall then have two days in which to make my arrangements and sink down out of sight in order to view the Coronation from the stand-point of the London beasts. That's all they are — beasts — if they are anything like the slum people of New York — beasts, shot through with stray flashes of divinity.
>
> I meet the men of the world, in the Pullman Coaches, New York clubs, and Atlantic-liner smoking rooms, and truth to say I am made more hopeful for the Cause by their total ignorance and non-understanding of the forces at work. They are blissfully ignorant of the coming upheaval, while they have grown bitterer and bitterer toward the workers. You see, the growing power of the workers is hurting them and making them bitter, while it does not open their eyes.[14]

What were the 'arrangements' he made? *The People of the Abyss* opens with an account of his going to the American Embassy and to Thomas Cook's for guidance in his projects, boarding a cab, and asking to be taken anywhere in the East End; then, without explanation of how it came about, going to the home of a plain-clothes policeman who apparently knew his mission and found him lodgings. The truth was not revealed for two reasons. One was Jack's eye for a striking opening to a story: to plunge by himself into the whirlpool was far more dramatic than to have been led to it by watchful friends. The other reason was the nature of his sponsorship. He was introduced to the East End by members of the Social Democratic Federation, the British marxist organisation. When his book was written he was uncertain of its acceptability for publication and decided (or was advised by Brett) that the basis had to be an individual's witness, without the taint — as many might say — of politics.

Almost certainly, he was put in touch by Anna. At the end of 1900 there is a reference in their correspondence to H.M. Hyndman, the leader of the Social Democratic Federation; he had praised some of Jack's work in a letter to her. A small group of SDF members were aware of Jack's visit and kept secret about it. His companion was one named Ernest Hunter, who later became a journalist on the *Daily Herald*; another was Edward Fairbrother. They supplied the official and medical reports on poverty and slum conditions that Jack cited. He remarked in *The People of the Abyss* on the change of people's attitudes when he was in down-and-out clothes; he would have found it near-impossible in that condition to get access to the books and papers he used. His lodgings were in Flower and Dean Street, in the heart of Jack the Ripper's terrain fifteen years before.[15] He dressed in shabby second-hand things bought in Stepney, and represented himself as a seaman. He slept in doss-houses ('I beg forgiveness of my body for the vileness through which I have dragged it, and forgiveness of my stomach for the vileness I have thrust into it'); he watched Edward VII's coronation procession, went to the hop-fields, walked the streets by day and night. He wrote to George and Carrie Sterling: 'I've read of misery, and seen a bit; but this beats anything I could even have imagined.' To Anna: 'I am made sick by this human hell-hole called the East End.' What horrified Jack most of all was the physique of the people. The slum-swellers of Britain were not 'beasts' as he had anticipated; they were underfed parodies of humanity.

It was a phenomenon which others besides him noticed. C.E. Montague in *Disenchantment*, that beautiful, compassionate book about the 1914-18 war, wrote of

battalions of colourless, stunted, half-toothless lads from

hot, humid Lancashire mills; battalions of slow, staring faces
... Dominions battalions of men startlingly taller, stronger,
handsomer; prouder; firmer in nerve, better schooled, more
boldly interested in life, quicker to take means to an end and
to parry and counter any new blow of circumstance, men
who had learned already to look at our men with the half-
curious, half-pitying look of a higher, happier caste at a
lower.

This was the nature of Jack's gaze at all those he met. The man
(possibly one of the SDF) who told him he weighed ten stone and
was considered a fine specimen: 'I was ashamed to tell him that I
weighed one hundred and seventy pounds, or over twelve stone, so
I contented myself with taking his measure. Poor, misshapen little
man!' And the incident of the two men who, walking with him,
picked up crusts and peel from the filthy pavement to eat: ' *and
this, between six and seven o'clock in the evening of August 20,
year of our Lord 1902, in the heart of the greatest, wealthiest and
most powerful empire the world has ever seen.* '
   The writing of *The People of the Abyss* was done while he was
still in the East End. The South Africa trip had been cancelled; he
sent his manuscript to the American Press Association, and before
returning to America travelled for a few weeks in Germany,
France and Italy. It was during this short period that he wrote the
only love-letters Bess ever received from him. She was several
months pregnant again, and renewed hope for a son surged
through Jack. The letters were tender and earnest; Bess in turn was
filled with hope that the future would be different. The child, born
in October, was another girl. On receiving the cable with the news
he started for home. Their marriage was almost over.
   The Press Association, regarding his manuscript as a
journalistic report, had submitted it for serial publication. Jack
wanted it for Macmillan's. He allowed the magazine enquiries to go
forward — it was eventually serialised in the radical monthly
Wilshire's for very low payment — but set to work revising the copy
he had and sent it to Brett for publication in book form. It was
everything Brett had believed it would be, and the American social
conscience was in tune to meet it. Brett was aware also of the
restrictions of that conscience. Offering a contract, he asked Jack
to make some modifications for the market. Of the final version,

Jack wrote:

> I have wholly cut out the references to the King of England in
> the Coronation chapter, have softened in a number of places,
> made it more presentable in many ways, and added a preface
> and a concluding chapter. (Letter to Brett, 16 February 1903)

The People of the Abyss established Jack's reputation as the
writer of the working class. It is undoubtedly the most, and perhaps
the only, truly sincere work he wrote. It is not a propagandist work,
except in the sense that to draw attention to an evil can in itself
provoke the demand for change. He existed in a slum-dweller's life,
sampling for himself its experiences, seeing the horrors at first
hand. Years later he said: 'Of all my books, I love most *The People
of the Abyss*. No other book of mine took so much of my young
heart and tears as that study of the economic degradation of the
poor.' For other socialists as well as for him the thought was
implicit that this cruelly-used mass must revolt as the downtrodden
mobs of France had done — 'crawl out of their dens and lairs' at
last to bring down their exploiters. Woe to the masters!

At this time too Jack's socialism was as fully formed as it
would ever be. In another two or three years his loss of faith was to
begin. Part of the process was his elevation, first as a prodigy and
then as a celebrity, by the socialists themselves. He began as the boy
socialist of Oakland, put on the platform and in the public eye
when an issue was to be created. The episode of his arrest for
violating the public-meeting laws when he was twenty-one has led
to the legend that he was a notable soap-box orator. In fact he was
ineffective — he lacked a carrying voice — and did not continue as
an outdoor speaker. The lectures and speeches he gave afterwards
were written and read out; some, including 'Revolution', became
his essays on socialism.

From the time his stories began to appear in the *Overland
Monthly* he was treated as a star in the Oakland and San Francisco
socialist parties. His growing reputation as a writer was used to
attract people to meetings and create prestige. It is understandable
why they should have done this, though it could have no beneficial
effect for them in the long run; they were working to establish the
movement, and anything which would be an attraction and bring
good repute was acceptable. The effect on Jack was disastrous. He

was put virtually beyond criticism, allowed to made declarations which from others might have been dismissed or condemned. His tendency in all things had been, once their nature was grasped, to place himself at the head and lay down laws. Now he could make pronouncements on society that were given precedence; his manner was to put down whoever opposed him as an inferior or a 'little person'.

Moreover, there was no uniformity of standpoint among the socialists. Some had broken with the Socialist Labour Party to go into the newly formed Socialist Party of America. Jack accompanied them but, significantly, the organisational argument on the split passed him by: he was his own man. Their outlooks ranged from Christian or ethical radicalism to Marxist materialism, from reformism to syndicalism. It was the case also that many people came to his lectures who were not interested in socialism at all, but wanted to see and rub shoulders with this exciting young writer. Jack enjoyed the adulation all the more when it came from those whom he felt to be his social superiors. One observer during this period, the socialist translator and writer Austin Lewis, wrote: 'The very frank admiration of the more honest, and the subtle flattery of the more sophisticated, each had its share in the production of a state of mind.'[16]

Jack was introduced to socialism while he was on the road. He related it immediately to what he was witnessing of social conditions, and what he had experienced. His idea of it was furthered by the Oakland meetings and discussions, and the talk in the Klondike log cabins. As always, he was invigorated by what he learned of Marx and 'the co-operative commonwealth'. Alongside socialism he took in other philosophies, each with its own kind of revelation. He did not balance them or consider the conflicts among them; rather, he viewed their statements as coming from intellectual giants who could co-exist. In addition he picked up ideas indiscriminately in his reading — often only phrases which meant little but appealed to him.

His use of philosophical phrases and references has masked the fact that he read relatively little of the thinkers he talked about. That is not to say he was a fraud. At the start he read carefully, digesting everything; as his hunger for knowledge grew he skimmed books, picking out items and believing he had the heart of the matter. No doubt his progress at the cramming academy and in studying for entrance to the university contributed to making him think this was how one learned; but he was always in haste, expecting to gain mastery overnight. Certainly an important part of his equipment was the facility, which he had to a high degree, of noting essentials and retaining and using them. For those whom he claimed as the founders of his social philosophy — Marx, Darwin, Spencer and Nietzsche — that was nothing like enough.

This is made plain by an examination of Jack's social and political essays. Despite their impressive language, many of the statements in them verge on absurdity or are meaningless. He had grasped the beginning of Marx's economic theory, that under capitalism the working class produces surplus value which is appropriated by the capitalists, but he could not understand how the surpluses were disposed of. 'The Question of the Maximum', which he wrote in 1898 and delivered repeatedly as a lecture until, revised, it was published in *Revolution and Other Essays*, is about this problem. In it, Jack proposes — to meet his own perplexity — that a critical point must soon be reached; the result will be either socialism or control by an 'oligarchy' whose raison d'être is to consume the surplus in non-productive works (the idea is repeated in *The Iron Heel*).

His most famous essay in socialism, 'Revolution', was acclaimed when he first gave it as a speech at the University of California in 1905. Yet its often-quoted opening contains an example of dramatically-rendered sloppy thinking which in its way characterises all Jack's political statements.

> I received a letter the other day. It was from a man in Arizona. It began, 'Dear Comrade'. It ended, 'Yours for the Revolution'. I replied to the letter, and my letter began, 'Dear Comrade'. It ended, 'Yours for the Revolution'. In the United States there are 400,000 men, of men and women nearly 1,000,000, who begin their letters 'Dear Comrade', and end them 'Yours for the Revolution'.

The passage goes on to claim numbers in Germany, France, Austria, Belgium, Italy, England, Switzerland, Denmark, Sweden, Holland, Spain — 'comrades all, and revolutionists'. Most commentators have observed, with hindsight, that he was letting his imagination run away with him. But the phrase 'of men and women nearly 1,000,000' represents a different kind of fallacy. Did Jack really believe that women revolutionaries substantially outnumbered men? He would have laughed at the idea; nevertheless, he was apparently saying so. The statement is simply meaningless, made for the sake of rhetorical effect.

Neither 'Revolution' nor *The Iron Heel* gives any explanation of socialism or how it is to be achieved. There are only metaphors of power: 'Here are our hands. They are strong hands. We are going to take your governments, your palaces, and all your purpled ease away from you ...' The case levelled against capitalism is not Marx's economic and historical one, or Spencer's doctrine of evolution, but is simply a charge of incompetence: 'The capitalist class, blind and greedy, grasping madly, has not only made the best of its management, but made the worst of it. It is a management prodigiously wasteful.' Only in the essay 'The Class Struggle' is there a definition of the purpose of the revolution and the manner of its taking place; and this is taken from the policy statement of the Socialist Party of America.

The strength of Jack's propagandist writing is his attacks on the evils of society in *The People of the Abyss*, in the early chapters of *The Iron Heel*, and in some essays and parts of his autobiographical books. He loved to be aggressive, and in this vein could be highly exhilarating. The condemnation of strikebreakers attributed to him is still cited today:

> After God had finished the rattlesnake, the toad and the vampire, he had some awful substance left with which He made a SCAB. A SCAB is a two-legged animal with a cork-screw soul, a water-logged brain, and a combination back-bone made of jelly and glue. Where others have hearts he carries a tumor of rotten principles. When a SCAB comes down the street men turn their backs and angels weep in heaven, and the devil shuts the gates of hell to keep him out. No man has a right to SCAB as long as there is a pool of water deep enough to drown his body in, or a rope long enough to hang his carcass with.[17]

The vigour of his kind of writing when it first appeared was in tune with the militancy of the growing labour movement in America —

— indeed, it reflects the mood of Kelly's Army and the hobos of the east. This was the difference between Jack and other writers who claimed to be socialists. Their criticisms of society were kept within the boundaries of discretion. His were made head-on, and publishers and the public liked it; it extended the full-bloodedness of his adventure stories.

Nevertheless, it concealed great deficiencies. Drawing attention to the evils of capitalism has always been nine-tenths of socialist propaganda; properly formulated, it makes an analysis from which the need and method of a fundamental change are drawn. Jack had no such analysis. He voiced what he had seen, identifying himself with the exploited and rebellious — not only by proclaiming himself a proletarian, but in his declared contempt for formal institutions of learning and 'the parlour floor of society'. But he did not understand how society worked; the virile, combative imagery concealed smatterings. The socialists' adulation and his quick rise to fame made him feel an oracle. His situation is unconsciously presented in his idealised portrait of himself as Ernest Everhard, the hero of *The Iron Heel*. Everhard's intellectual strength is shown in a series of discussions in which he crushes his opponents with seeming omniscience; in fact they are accessories, feeding lines for Jack's rhetorical responses.

The other element which dominated Jack's social thinking was his conviction of racial superiority. It may have begun in his boyhood with Flora's snobbishness, or its elements been discovered somewhere in his juvenile reading. Certainly it was fostered by his admiration of Kipling; but the true formative force was Benjamin Kidd's *Social Evolution*. Almost forgotten now, it was a widely read popularisation of Herbert Spencer; it was published in 1894, and its influence was sufficient for Arthur M. Lewis to name Kidd as one of the subjects of his *Ten Blind Leaders of the Blind*. [18] Its argument was from the principle of the survival of the fittest, applied to society. 'This orderly and beautiful world which we see around us now is, and always has been,' Kidd wrote, 'the scene of incessant rivalry between all the forms of life inhabiting it — rivalry, too, not chiefly conducted between different species but between members of the same species.'

Kidd asserted that this rivalry was the key to progress. He rejected socialism though it was 'the truthful, unexaggerated teaching of sober reason', because it would suspend the struggle for existence. The interests of the exploited class must be subordinate to the interests of the race; and the strongest, highest representative of the race was the Anglo-Saxon. Jack was profoundly impressed. It is possible that his reverence for Herbert Spencer was gained through Kidd. Curiously, he refrained from mentioning him, perhaps because Kidd was condemned by Marxists as a reactionary; but he borrowed repeatedly from him — Jack's essay 'The Shrinkage of the Planet', written in 1900, has a phrase of Kidd's for its title.

In 1899 Jack was laying down Anglo-Saxon superiority to Cloudesley Johns in successive letters. Johns must have dissented on various counts, for Jack replied calling upon a transcendental logic which he termed 'the law'. He spoke first of women, for whom 'the law' meant that economic and political independence were made impossible by the need to be subservient to men. As regards race and socialism, the logic — which 'petty worms of men must bow to' — was:

> Socialism is not an ideal system, devised by man for the happiness of all life; nor for the happiness of all men; but it is devised for the happiness of certain kindred races. It is devised so as to give more strength to these certain kindred favoured races so that they may survive and inherit the earth to the extinction of the lesser, weaker races. The very men who advocate socialism, may tell you of the brotherhood of all men, and I know they are sincere; but that does not alter the law — they are simply instruments, working blindly for the betterment of these certain kindred races, and working detriment to the inferior races they would call brothers.

It was almost pure Kidd, and it was an outlook Jack was to retain to the end of his life. In his last year he repeated still more dogmatically to a correspondent who had challenged him:

> Consult the entire history of the human world in all past ages, and you will find that the world has ever belonged to the pure breed, and has never belonged to the mongrel. I give you this as a challenge: Read up your history of the human race. Remember, Nature permits no mongrel to live — or, rather, Nature permits no mongrel to endure ... You will find it all

there on the shelves. And find me one race that has retained its power of civilisation, culture, and creativeness, after it mongrelised itself.[19]

Occasionally, during the fairly short period when he was optimistic about socialism, he spoke differently. In 'Revolution' he said the socialist camaraderie 'passes over geographical lines, transcends race prejudice'. The few faint flourishes of this sort were perhaps acknowledgements of the goodwill the radical movement bore him; but his conviction never altered that the Anglo-Saxons must inherit the earth. In 1904 he produced an article called 'The Yellow Peril' — it was, incongruously, included in the collection *Revolution and Other Essays* — repeating that the Saxon represented ethical superiority: 'we are a right-seeking race'.

It would be unfair not to consider some influences of the time. A good deal of the knowledge which makes enlightenment about race possible today was not available then. In *Ten Blind Leaders of the Blind*, Arthur Lewis pointed out that Kidd wrote his book prior to the appearances of Kropotkin's *Mutual Aid* and De Vries' *Mutation*; had he seen them his theories would have been modified, in Lewis's opinion. The founders of socialist theory had themselves been uncertain about race. A letter from Frederick Engels to a student, Starkenburg, in 1894 said: 'We regard economic conditions as the factor which ultimately determines historical development. But race is itself an economic factor.' Plekhanov's *Fundamental Problems of Marxism*, written about the same time, is hopeful but uncertain that races are equal.[20]

A further aspect was the repeated controversies over immigration to the United States. There had been a surge of 'nativism' at the beginning of the second half of the nineteenth century, directed first against Irish 'Papists' and then against immigrants from southern and eastern Europe; Flora London's racial pride came from this source. And in California, Chinese immigration was a dominant political issue from 1860 onwards. Though the basic issues were entirely economic, racial allegations made the everyday arguments: the Chinese were charged with being unassimilable and full of vice. When Jack sailed the Bay with the oyster-pirates and as a fish-patrolman, the Chinese fishermen were fair game for everyone.

Nevertheless, Jack held something more than a common share

of prejudice. Kidd's teaching appealed to him because it affirmed his view of himself. He had been a child who was never a child, knowing little of co-operative play; he found and achieved everything alone. A free agent, he had consumed but never shared experience. In groups he was always apart, at first the outsider seeking acceptance and then — quickly — finding himself the others' superior. In his adventures he had demanded supremacy as of right, and won it. He had worked harder and sailed better than anyone else; beaten the students at their learning game; matched the Indians at packing over the snowbound northern hills.

Marxism would have taught him the interaction between men and their social environment: Jack London was the product of the forces of his time. Yet, almost by definition, the explanation could not have satisfied him. It had to be that he was of an imperial minority for whom the world was made. Perversely, of course, the fact was that if William Chaney was his father he had not a shred of Anglo-Saxon descent. Perhaps he made an added cause from it; if blood did not prove him to belong to the highest of the favoured races, achievement would. That these beliefs could co-exist with socialism has always been viewed as impossible. However, their synthesis was what made 'Jack London socialism' most attractive: a red-blooded call to action, a reiteration that Jack had no time for those who did not stand up and fight. In his mind only the fittest would do so and survive the final clash with the masters of society. It was the law.

7. Success and Charmian

While Jack was in Europe three books by him had been published: *A Daughter of the Snows, The Children of the Frost,* and *The Cruise of the Dazzler.* Their appearance in a single month was a record, and also drew attention to the way he had been working. *A Daughter of the Snows* was received tolerantly but without enthusiasm: the reputation his other work had established stopped any critic describing it as what it was, a first novel of poor quality. *The Cruise of the Dazzler* was unashamedly a pot-boiler, a light adventure story for boys. But *Children of the Frost* made a strong mark. It was praised even more than *The Son of the Wolf* had been. There were no more comparisons with other writers. Jack was recognised now as having set his own standard in telling stories — 'a domain which is his by right of conquest', as one reviewer wrote.

George Brett saw that there were huge differences in the quality of the three books because Jack had worked to excess, forcing his output in search of a market. The published work did not represent a steady development but was drawn from a stock produced over the preceding three years — indeed, Jack had almost exhausted this stock and contemplated an intensive bout of writing to replenish it. Brett's advice to him was: 'I hope that your work from this time will show the marks of advancement which I found so strong in your earlier books, but which is not so marked in the last volume or so, these showing signs of haste.' Jack acknowledged that this was his situation. In a long reply to Brett he described himself as a slow writer: 'The reason I have turned out so much is because I have worked constantly, day in and day out, without taking a rest.'[21]

Macmillan proposed a financial arrangement which would

end the necessity for hurried writing and allow him to concentrate on 'the best a man can do', as Brett put it. Two weeks after his return to California, Jack sent the revised manuscript of *The Kempton-Wace Letters* and a full account of his financial position and his plans. He wanted to get away from the Klondike: that had provided the apprenticeship he had now served. He had in mind a novel to be called *The Flight of the Duchess*[22] and a sea story, together with some short stories based on his Fish-Patrol days. Including *The People of the Abyss*, he would have six books in Brett's hands in the next twelve months. He proposed that, against these, Macmillan's pay him $150 a month — a sum which would support him and his family while he devoted himself to 'larger and more ambitious work'.

They accepted Jack's proposition, and extended the initial period to two years. To be released from hack writing was of supreme importance. The 'apprenticeship' of which he spoke had been hectic and could not have continued much longer without some change of course. But for Brett's wisdom Jack might well have been bought by *McClure's,* the *Cosmopolitan* or one of the other magazines which were building huge circulations by sensational reportage and exposures. As it was, he was enabled to reflect on what he always termed 'big books'. He was expecting further rewards from the publication of his books abroad. A London firm, Isbister & Co., had undertaken to bring them out in England (in fact Isbister's failed early in 1904, and the total of Jack's receipts from them was £10).

The Kempton-Wace Letters was published in May 1903. Brett had been less than wholeheartedly keen on it — in all likelihood he regarded it as a side-venture to be tolerated because of the other work he expected. Jack urged him that the book had good chances of success: 'We are given more to an analysis of our emotions these days than ever before, while the tendency of the American reading public is so strong towards things scientific, that a scientific discussion of love is bound to arouse interest.' Published anonymously, it was received better than Brett had expected; the reviewers found it 'unusual' and, as Jack had presaged, in keeping with the enquiring mood of the time. A San Francisco journalist — perhaps he had been to the socialist lectures — recognised Jack's passion for the evolutionary process and his turns of phrase, and by the time a second edition was printed the authors' names were known.

The Kempton-Wace Letters is a novel, telling a story through the exchange of letters. The extent to which they represent a real debate between Anna Strunsky and Jack is small. Explaining them to Johns, he wrote:

> A young Russian Jewess of 'Frisco and myself have often quarrelled over our conception of love. She happens to be a genius. She is also a materialist by philosophy, and an idealist by innate preference, and is constantly being forced to twist all the facts of the universe in order to reconcile herself with herself. So, finally, we decided that the only way to argue the question out would be by letter. Then we wondered if a collection of letters should happen to be worth publishing.[23]

Besides indicating that he had not told Johns anything of Anna — he had known her for almost a year — this shows what the substance of the *Letters* was. The conflict in them is not between his and her outlooks, but devised from contradictions which he attributed to her alone. Lacking sophistication, Anna apparently accepted the false position. She might — indeed, should — have argued that a materialist philosophy does not at all exclude or devalue emotional life. Instead, she is found defending romantic love against a clinical posture which Jack alleged to be that of the scientific materialist.

Neither of them was arguing from conviction. Anna's letters are eloquent pleas for the heart to have its way; Jack's are a platform for statements about the survival of the fittest and eugenic principles. One view has been that they were a rationale for his marriage to Bess. However, while he was at work on the *Letters* the marriage was far from well, and shortly after the book's completion he wrote to Johns: 'It's all right for a man sometimes to marry philosophically, but remember it's damned hard on the woman.' It was Anna, not he, who was the centre of the book. He was more than half in love with her, and the prolonged discussion of feelings was an amorous exploration. Besides that, she 'happened to be a genius'. The remark was a declaration of where Jack had come to find his greatest satisfaction in standing: acknowledging others' intellectual and social superiority, while having it understood that in exposition of the laws of life he was their master.

He wrote a dog story while publication of the *Letters* and *The People of the Abyss* was awaited. He had promised Macmillan's one more book of Klondike pieces, and this was intended as a companion to his story 'Batard'. Writing to Anna and to Brett, he said it had run away with him; he had intended 4,000 words, but it grew to 42,000. Naming it *The Call of the Wild*, he sent it to the *Saturday Evening Post* for serial publication and Macmillan's for publication as a book. Neither he nor the publishers liked the title, and all tried to think of something better: the *Post* proposed to re-name it 'The Wolf'. Indeed Brett, though he thought the story a masterpiece, was doubtful whether it would be appreciated by the public. Animal stories were always popular, but they had to be sentimental — the market was for Seton-Thompson's tales and books like *Black Beauty*. Brett offered two thousand dollars to buy it outright, and Jack accepted. The *Saturday Evening Post* paid him seven hundred dollars. For a month's work, it seemed a remarkable reward; yet *The Call of the Wild* has sold over six million copies.

In fact it was an immediate success. The first edition of ten thousand was sold out on the first day, and reviewers poured out praise for its prose qualities as well as the magnificence of the story. Conspicuously, it was more than a gripping narrative; John L. Hervey spoke of 'its profound implications and their artistic embodiment by the reader who reads for other than the story.' *The Call of the Wild*'s achievement was due partly to the break Jack had had in his trip to Europe, which freshened his mind before he returned to the Klondike theme. But the 'profound implications' were of a human allegory. There was the struggle for existence, taken from the city scene where he had recently witnessed it to a cold primitive world; there was also his own emergence by strength alone from a poverty-stricken background to superiority over others.

How much Jack had such allegory in mind in writing *The Call of the Wild* is unsure. He professed afterwards to have been unconscious of it: 'I did not mean to do it.' That seems improbable — the more so since he began immediately afterwards to develop the theme in a human context, and recall the subject in the title, in *The Sea Wolf*. Yet he treated *The Call of the Wild* as simply a story which had struck lucky; the same might have happened to any other piece of work. Nor did he resent that it was a gold-mine to the publishers. He saw that Brett had taken a chance, and had made little from *The Kempton-Wace Letters*. The two thousand seven hundred dollars, on top of his regular payments from Macmillan, was money to pay bills and to spend. He bought a boat called the *Spray* and went sailing in the Bay and along the rivers while he wrote.

His marriage ended in this summer when success came. The last home he had gone to with Bess, in February 1902, was a house at Piedmont. It had big rooms and stood in five acres of wooded grounds; there was 'a most famous porch, broad and long and cool', a view of the whole of San Francisco Bay, and a cottage for Flora and Johnny Miller. After writing *The Call of the Wild* Jack began entertaining lavishly again: a hundred people a week came, the majority of them to the Wednesday open-house when they crowded the huge living room. Jack was paying two servants, and Mammy Jenny came to look after the children, but Bess did not like this kind of life and could not fit into it. She lacked the energy to organise the continual supplies of food, and had not the inclination to dress as Jack wished or to join in the games and chatter. She did not understand why he wanted to be surrounded by friends and praised. Most of all, she was jealous of the women who came and the way he enjoyed their attention.

Although Jack wrote later 'She feared every woman ... Jealous of everybody ... Bessie was suspicious of everybody', it is quite clear that she had ample reasons. Soon after their misconceived marriage he had been, as he now admitted, 'tangled up with Anna Strunsky'. Away from Oakland, he had pursued the doctrine of 'I like'. On his journey across America to meet Brett and go to London in 1902, he met a woman on the train. 'Let me tell you a little affair which will indicate the ease with which I let loose the sexual man. You will remember when I started for South Africa. In my car was travelling a woman with a maid and a child. We came together on the jump, at the very start, and had each other clear to Chicago. It was sexual passion, clear and simple ... Nothing remained when our three days and nights were over.' [24]

Luxuriating in success, in the pleasures of scattering money and being flattered, Jack found in Bess's aversions and her failure to give him a son the justification for doing as he liked. The Wednesday parties were given more and more to noisy romping, full of horseplay and practical jokes; there were picnics in the grounds, when squealing girls threw fruit and chased Jack, and pails of water were flung. In a subsequent letter going over the summer's happenings, Jack described a typical afternoon picnic:

> I remember the Sunday very well. I spent a great deal of time — practically all the time — while Joaquin was present getting drunk, in fooling with the girls. I washed Kate's face with cherries and dirt, if you will remember, and it took some time, all that squabbling around with Kate. I poured a lot of water over Charmian; also, when Carlt and Charmian got to fooling with the box of powder, Carlt threw the box of powder into the brush, and I spent a good while getting said box out of the brush.[25]

It was all interspersed with card-playing, flying box-kites, reciting, piano-playing and singing. One can perceive in it Jack's search for the childhood he never had; and the persistent sexual closeness with girls whom he half-despised. He said he had made up his mind 'to deliberately and intentionally go to pieces' that summer. But he was working steadily; it was not his own break-up, but that of his domestic life, he was encouraging to happen.

In June Bess took the two baby girls for a holiday at Glen Ellen, in Sonoma County. They were staying in one of a group of cabins belonging to Mrs Eames of the *Overland Monthly*. Jack proposed to sail in the *Spray* before going to join them — professedly to work on *The Sea Wolf*, in fact 'to have a hell of a time with any woman I could get hold of'. He eyed, as one likely partner, Charmian Kittredge: 'she was a warm enough proposition to suit me in an illicit way'. Before he had made his move, he drove into town with some friends: the horse-drawn carriage lost a wheel, and Jack's knee was hurt in the upset. Charmian came to help, and they talked and kissed. When Jack, his sailing cancelled by the accident, went to Glen Ellen he wrote to her and went to see her: 'I was growing more desirous of her, and more desirous for her to become my mistress.'[26]

He was still on the loose, however. While he viewed Charmian, he took out another man's wife and arranged to go with her on a steamboat voyage. Bess did not know in detail what was happening, but she guessed its nature. When a telegram about the boat trip came, she insisted on seeing it; she pieced together a torn-up typewritten letter to Jack, learning everything except that it came from Charmian. She was deeply disturbed by the publication of *The Kempton-Wace Letters*, finding significance in the effusiveness of its phrases about love. She asked Jack if he loved someone else; not caring about the pain he inflicted, he said he did.

The parting came one day near the end of July, at Glen Ellen. Sitting by a stream, Jack asked Bess if she would be willing to go and live on a ranch in the South California Desert, where he could work uninterrupted. She agreed. A few hours later he came to her in the cabin and said he was separating from her. He would not discuss it, and left in the morning. Though she knew that he was seeing other women, Bess was shattered. Like his letters from Europe, the talk of South California had roused hope in her of a fresh start. She did not dream that he and Charmian had been exchanging letters whose ardent terms make plain that they were lovers now.

There was a special reason why Bess did not suspect the truth. Jack returned to Piedmont, cleared his personal possessions from the house, and moved Flora and Johnny into a flat in Oakland while he stayed on the *Spray*. Charmian befriended Bess, went to the house and sat consoling her. A letter to Jack in September said: 'Last night I went to see Bessie. She was lovely to me — so lovely it made me sick. She begged me to come and stay all night with her, any time. She was so sweet and hospitable that it seemed as if all the trouble and tearing apart might be a dream. Sometimes I have to fight off a feeling of actual WICKEDNESS when I think of it all, but my reason enters and helps me, but oh!!!' Bess's other and more permanent ally was, unexpectedly, Flora. Pushed into the background when Jack married, treated generously but slightingly, she had been resentful of Bess. Now she came forward to condemn Jack for abandoning his family, and remained their friend for the rest of her life.

What kind of people were these? Like unthinking greedy children, they were determined that what they wanted must be theirs. Jack was not insensitive, and undoubtedly was deeply troubled — his proposal to go to South California must have been a half-hearted last attempt to turn away from the direction in which his impulses were pulling. He had come increasingly to dislike Bess for her narrowness. He expressed little compunction over the parting, and a month after it he wrote to Johns: 'I laugh when I think of what a hypocrite I was, when, at the Bungalow, I demanded from you your long-deferred congratulations for my marriage — but, believe me, I was a hypocrite grinning on a grid.' As soon as their separation was confirmed hostility blazed on both sides; he wrote her long vindictive letters, and continued to abuse her until his death. Yet the catastrophe had started in the same precipitate assertion of his wants that he was showing now. Impatient to realise an ambition, he had pressed Bess into a hasty marriage on terms which virtually foredoomed it; he was in love with Anna and had no intention of giving her up — or, as he had written of himself, of exercising any restraint 'when it happens to clash with desire'.

His concern and unhappiness were over the children. Disappointed as he was that they were girls, fatherhood meant a great deal to him. Soon after the parting he learned that Joan was ill with typhoid. He rushed home and stayed almost continuously at the child's bedside, promising anything if she should get well; the story went round that Jack and his wife were reconciled. Joan recovered, and he went away. It is impossible to comprehend or judge Jack London, however, without reference to his childhood which lacked stability or affection. He had discovered not only worlds of adult fantasy but, repeatedly, that by cutting strings he could make the fantasies come true almost immediately. 'Duty' meant only financial support and the need to work. He applied it now. He sent money regularly to Bess and accepted all the bills. If he worked harder and longer, providing and giving security, his duty was performed in the way it had been in his boyhood; he could believe no other responsibility existed.

Charmian Kittredge had a different background. In 1903 she was thirty-two, five years older than Jack. Her parents were dead and she had been brought up in San Francisco by her aunt, Ninetta Eames. She worked as a shorthand-typist in a shipping office, and helped with the *Overland Monthly*. She was a young woman of the new generation: capable, unconventional, and possessed of unusual vitality and courage. Photographs confirm that she was not pretty, but she had an attractive figure and had learned to dress to the best advantage. She read widely and talked well, played the piano, and rode; she went regularly to the Londons' house on horseback through the woods. Why Charmian had not married is something of a mystery. Some commentators have claimed that she talked a little too eagerly and laughed a little too loudly, making her desire to find a husband over-conspicuous; Jack's seeing her as 'a warm enough proposition' suggests that.

She and Jack first met in 1900, when he was writing his stories for the *Overland Monthly*. He visited the Eames home two or three times, and had arranged to go out with her in the week when he married Bess Maddern. He mentioned her in a letter to Johns: 'Have made the acquaintance of Charmian Kittredge, a charming girl who writes book reviews, and who possesses a pretty little library wherein I have found all these late books which the public libraries are afraid to have circulated.' After his marriage she went for a fifteen months' trip to the eastern states and Europe; subsequently she became a visitor to their home and a participant in the parties. Charmian was convinced that Jack was mismated. The thought was Mrs Eames's. A fulsome, pushful woman, she had half-planned her niece's union with Jack. When he wrote telling her of his sudden decision to marry, she bewailed it as a calamitous mistake from which no good would come. She seems to have continued to eye the situation shrewdly, ready to interfere when the opportunity presented itself and treating Jack as their protégé. Charmian, under her influence and strongly attracted to Jack, was never far from ready for whatever approach he might make.

When she was revealed as Jack's lover, Charmian was criticised by most of his friends. She was blamed and belittled for the rest of her life: one of the motifs of *Sailor on Horseback* is disparagement of her. Nor did the publication of their love-letters, in her biography, reduce the disfavour. It was a courageous mistake. These letters in which each tried to outdo the other in purple adolescent language only affirmed to their readers that Jack London, the master of realism, had been led into an unworthy infatuation. Certainly it is true that Charmian and Jack acted discreditably and deceitfully. What can be said is that if it had not been Charmian it would have been somebody else: who, in all probability, would not have been as successful at being married to

Jack as she was.

Their relationship rested, as she understood from the start, on her complete compliance with him. In the biography there is a telling incident from the period while they awaited his divorce from Bess. Jack, staying with Charmian and her aunt, was under the depression he called 'the Long Sickness'. They urged him to leave the *Spray* and spend the summer at Glen Ellen, but he refused — the quiet would drive him mad.

> 'Very well, then', I gave up, with my best cheer; 'the thing for you is to do what you feel you must, of course. And we won't say any more about it.'
>
> He started, flushed, turned and looked at me. Reaching for my hand, in a hushed, changed tone that meant volumes, he breathed:
>
> 'Why — why — you're a woman in a million.'

Charmian learned to play cards as well as to sail, boxed with him, typed his work and read proofs. She had to learn also to follow his moods, never to interrupt him, not to play the piano except when he requested it. He allowed her no financial independence, refusing her a separate bank account or even an 'allowance' and insisting that money should be spent by him alone. She had to conceal any problem of her own. When she had borne and lost their baby in 1910, for two or three years she was obliged to hide ill-health — he had made plain that he had no sympathy for female disorders. Likewise, before their marriage he wrote to her: 'One thing I want to tell you for your own good and our happiness together. I do not think you are a hysterical woman. But don't ever have hysterics with me.'

Above all, it was his sexual allegiance that she held. The earliest of their letters, written before he told Bess he was leaving, convey how Charmian had shown a passionate generosity which Jack had only imagined until then: 'Had you been coy and fluttering, giving the lie to what you had already appeared to be by manifesting the slightest prudery or false fastidiousness, I really think I should have been utterly disgusted.' The love-letters he continued to write to her over the years dwelt on physical qualities — horsemanship, swimming, the 'grit' she undoubtedly had. In 1914, from New York, he wrote of his preoccupation with 'your sweet, beautiful body'; their address to each other was 'Mate-man' and 'Mate-woman'.

It was not simply that he demanded strong sexual satisfactions. He virtually rejected any other kind of relationship with a woman, believing his ventures in 'spiritual' love with Mabel and contractual affection with Bess to have proved the fraudulence of such ideas. To a woman who wrote in 1910, protesting against his treatment of relationships in *Martin Eden*, he wrote;

> I was no more treacherous to Martin Eden than life is treacherous to many, many men and women ... from what I know of love, I believe that Martin Eden had his first big genuine love when he fell in love with Ruth, and that not he alone, but countless millions of men and women, have been tricked in one way or another in similar fashion.

He could understand and be loyal to love as a physical effusion. When it took more complex forms, requiring emotional self-surrender, it eluded and bewildered Jack until in anger he declared it to be all a delusion. There was another element in his dedication to Charmian: he disliked women. At some stage he knew men sexually. Charmian was aware of this. She referred to 'abnormalities of his early rough days', and in a long introspective letter to her early in their marriage he wrote: 'I have experienced the greater frankness, several times, under provocation, with a man or two, and a woman or two.' His desire for 'the great Man-Comrade' persisted and was made more explicit in his relationship with George Sterling; but the combination of sturdy athleticism and keen sexuality in Charmian seems to have provided a satisfaction for the homosexual yearnings Jack undoubtedly had.

Separation from Bess made him short of money once more. *The People of the Abyss* came out in November to be acclaimed everywhere. Johns came and stayed on the *Spray* with him and he sent the first half of *The Sea Wolf* to Macmillan. Brett was thrilled with it, and contacted the *Century* magazine to propose its serialisation. *Century* offered four thousand dollars for the finished work — far more than *The Call of the Wild* had brought Jack, and before the finances of publication as a book had been even discussed. Yet, in the meantime, his income was unspectacular and practically all of it went to Bess. He had done some hack work for *Youth's Companion* and other papers to bring in ready money. A week before Christmas he had only twenty dollars in the bank.

The outbreak of war between Russia and Japan as 1904 began suggested an opportunity for a change of surroundings and some well-paid journalism. He made known that he was available, and quickly received offers: 'Could have gone for *Harper's, Collier's* and N.Y.Herald', he wrote to Johns, 'but Hearst made the best offer.' He left San Francisco for Yokohama on 7 January among several other correspondents. He was seen off by 'The Crowd'. *The Sea Wolf* had been completed in a final spurt and despatched to the *Century* the previous day; Charmian and George Sterling were entrusted with the proof-reading. Five days after Jack sailed 'The Crowd' assembled again, at the Sterlings' home, to drink Jack's health on his twenty-eighth birthday.

There was another event on the day of the sailing that he did not know about. Bess, certain that Jack had another woman, had been casting about frantically to learn her identity. She confided in Charmian and Flora, and asked Eliza Shepard to help. Eliza knew that Jack trusted her. She said she would go aboard the steamer to bid him goodbye, and she promised Bess: 'And I know that I shall there discover who the woman is.' She did; and Jack sailed through the Golden Gate looking forward to a new adventure, unaware that Bess had been told.

8. The Individualist

The war-correspondent journey was a series of misfortunes and errors. The sea voyage promised to be carefree, but Jack first had influenza and then sprained an ankle so badly that he could barely walk when they reached Yokohama. He went by train to Tokyo, where the correspondents were being entertained by officials; and quickly learned that the Japanese government in fact aimed to keep foreign journalists away from the fighting.

Determined to make his way to where the troops were massing, Jack began a series of fruitless journeys by train and steamer. He wrote to Charmian frequently and sent cables and photographs to Hearst. His plan was to travel to the Manchurian battlefront from Korea, but he moved repeatedly from one town to another as passages were cancelled. He was seen taking pictures in Moji and arrested on suspicion of being a spy; his camera was confiscated. Eventually he chartered a junk — the Korean coast, with wild landscapes appearing between snow squalls, was to be described in *The Star Rover.* In some of the villages where the junk stopped he was the first white man to be seen; the special curiosity was his false teeth, which he displayed again and again. His journey was filled with hardship from intense cold, and the lingering effects of influenza and his ankle injury; an English journalist who saw him at one point described him as a physical wreck.

Just before the end of February he got to Seoul. The war had been on for two weeks now. Though other correspondents had passed through, the military authorities seemed to have no instructions about Jack. He hired two horses, three pack-ponies, a Japanese interpreter, and three Koreans to cook and look after the horses, and set out for the battle lines. He arrived at Siu-Wan, the farthest point north reached by any journalist, after two weeks' riding; and he was at once sent back. He retreated only a little way, to Ping-yang, but the Japanese authoritites insisted that he return to Seoul. The pressure came, ironically, from the batch of journalists still held in Tokyo. Protesting against their detention, they pointed out that some correspondents had been permitted, apparently, to go ahead; the Japanese response was to order all correspondents back.

Jack kicked his heels in hotels for a month, watching columns of soldiers go by and creaking bullock-carts loaded with supplies. His clothes had lice in them; his hatred of yellow men grew. He tried to ride north again, and was confronted by Japanese guards pointing bayonets. He was assigned to the First Column of the Japanese army with some other newspapermen, but not allowed to proceed. He sent dispatches, commenting: 'Perfect rot I am turning out. It's not war correspondence at all, and the Japs are not allowing us to see any war.' He gave a reading from *The Call of the Wild* to the YMCA in Seoul, wearing evening dress. April gave way to May, and Jack wrote to Hearst that he would return home unless arrangements could be made for him to go to the Russian side.

Before the question could be seriously considered, his anger produced the incident which made his return to the United States obligatory. Each of the correspondents had servants, including a groom. There were continual squabbles among these boys over the fodder rations. Jack intervened in one of the disputes; his boy alleged that another had been stealing their food, and Jack lost his temper and knocked the other boy down. The matter was serious. The other journalists armed themselves while Jack was arrested and taken before General Fuji, the chief of staff. There was talk of a court martial and execution. Richard Harding Davis, one of the correspondents still in Tokyo, cabled to the American President, Theodore Roosevelt. Jack was released, but he had to return to Tokyo and leave Japan immediately. He was accompanied to Yokohama and the ship by Davis.

Despite his frustration, Jack had done better than any other correspondent. The Hearst press had published his dispatches and photographs, and found his anti-Japanese sentiments thoroughly acceptable. Others were shocked by them. One of the war correspondents, Edwin Emerson Jr,[27] asserted that a man who 'according to his own professions, loathed and abominated the

Japanese' was unsuitable for the assignment. The most astonished and hurt of all, of course, were his fellow socialists. They knew that Hearst was campaigning against 'the yellow peril' and demanding the exclusion of Asiatics from the United States, but had not dreamed that an ardent preacher for the co-operative common-wealth would feed this racism. There was an incredible affront in dispatches such as the one in which Jack described his reaction to seeing Russian prisoners who were blue-eyed and white: 'These men were my kind ... my place was there inside with them in their captivity rather than outside in freedom among the aliens.'

A breach between Jack London and his comrades in the socialist movement was clearly in sight. Indeed, it should have taken place. The struggle against racial discrimination was high on their programme, and their complaisance towards his statements and actions is itself more than a little shocking. Attempts were made to challenge him when he went over his Japanese experiences in a lecture at the Oakland headquarters and 'cursed the entire yellow race in the most outrageous terms'. Members pointed to the slogan on the wall: 'Workers of all countries, unite!' Jack's answer to their criticism was to pound the table and assert loudly: 'I am first of all a white man and only then a socialist!' In his home he was displaying something almost as remarkable as his declarations. He had brought home a Korean servant-boy. His many visitors found the boy not only cleaning and waiting at table, but dressing Jack and calling him 'Master'. Jack justified it easily, praising Manyoungi's 'spirit of service' and asking: 'Why tie my own shoes when I can have it done by someone whose business it is, while I am improving my mind or entertaining the fellows who drop in?'

A number of socialists cooled towards him, and when he moved from Oakland a year later several of his associations virtually ceased. However, they did not publicly repudiate or disown his views. His value as a figurehead over-rode the repugnance his attitudes roused. In Jack's last years he criticised the leaders of the socialist movement for their compromises. The charge was accurate; but it should have extended back to the time when too many eyes closed half-wilfully to his own denial of the brotherhood of man. Austin Lewis told Joan London in the nineteen-thirties: 'In 1899, Jack stood with one foot planted in the soil of social-democracy, but the other foot was already being clogged in the morasses of the philosophical teachings from which have sprung fascism.' Lewis was always frank with Jack, but others failed to be frank with either the movement or themselves.

Jack's reputation as a writer grew and his private life became more entangled. Before he disembarked on 30 June 1904, he was served with divorce papers and notice that an attachment for maintenance had been placed on his earnings and possessions. He had wanted the divorce proceedings to begin; but, to his dismay, Anna Strunsky was named as co-respondent. Though Bess had been told that Jack was now involved with Charmian, she believed it was Anna who had undermined their marriage. She did not allege adultery, but that Jack's association with Anna — in particular, the collaboration in *The Kempton-Wace Letters* — had made him indifferent to his wife. The story was in newspapers all over America. Anna had left San Francisco before the *Letters* were published and was now in New York; when reporters visited her she replied that the allegations were 'merely vulgar'.

Jack wrote begging forgiveness, but he was anxious to keep Charmian's name out of the case. She had been staying in the east, and confessed herself frightened of the scandal. He went to Bess to bargain, pointing out that if they struggled over money the beneficiaries would be only the lawyers. He agreed on his part to build a house in Piedmont for her and the children, and she on her part to change her grounds for divorce to simple desertion. He stayed in a cottage belonging to Ninetta Eames at Glen Ellen, writing long letters to try to coax Charmian there, and went sailing in the *Spray*.

Another collection of Klondike stories, *The Faith of Men*, was published and quickly reprinted. *The Sea Wolf* had a tremendous impact as a magazine serial and Macmillan, preparing its book publication, reported advance sales of 20,000. Though he was mentally tired and physically sick — a nervous skin irritation plagued him as well as another bout of influenza — Jack went on turning out all the work he could, needing more and more money. He produced *The Game*, a short novel about a prizefighter, and worked at a play derived from one of his stories, 'The Scorn of Women'. The money from the *Century* and from Hearst went to buying land and starting Bess's house. At his request, Brett had increased his monthly advances to $250; part of this went to Bess and the children, lawyers' bills were coming in, and there was his undiminished desire to be seen living well and entertaining friends. He wrote to Brett suggesting new editions of his earlier works, and outlining further plans.

The Sea Wolf created a sensation. Written with all Jack's realism, it combined brutal adventure with an intellectual theme. Wolf Larsen sprang to life as one of the most extraordinary of all fictional characters — Nietzsche's superman, living by harsh physical force yet given to philosophy and poetry. Against him were posed the two lovers who also represented reason, which Larsen brushed aside. The dramatic appeal was that of a more vivid *Dr Jekyll and Mr Hyde*, or Dickens's *Edwin Drood*: the conflict between two elements in man. Another fascination of the book was its popularisation of philosophical ideas and phrases. Millions were excited by Larsen's self-justifications — 'Better to reign in hell than serve in heaven', and 'Might is right'.

In later years Jack insisted on a deeper meaning for *The Sea Wolf*: that it was part of a confutation of individualism. In 1915, in a letter to the writer Mary Austin, he said:

> Long years ago, at the beginning of my writing career, I attacked Nietzsche and his super-man idea. This was in *The Sea Wolf*. Lots of people read *The Sea Wolf,* no one discovered that it was an attack upon the super-man philosophy. Later on, not mentioning my shorter efforts, I wrote another novel that was an attack upon the super-man idea, namely my *Martin Eden*. No one discovered that this was such an attack.

There is an enormous self-revelation in this statement. In fact he had not read Nietzsche when he wrote *The Sea Wolf*. According to Charmian he first read *Thus Spake Zarathustra* and *Genealogy of Morals* while she was typing the play 'Scorn of Women' for him; he was enthusiastic and immediately commended Nietzsche to her, and they read and discussed the other works. This would have been in the middle and later months of 1904, some time after the completion of *The Sea Wolf*. Before then he had picked up Nietzsche's phrases, and constructed images from them, through listening to Strawn-Hamilton and others: 'blond beast', 'the superman', 'live dangerously.'.

Obviously Jack did not repudiate individualism — on the

contrary, the period when *The Sea Wolf* was written and published was one in which he asserted personal wilfulness and his conviction of Anglo-Saxon superiority more strongly than ever before. Nietzscheanism appears as a decoration of Wolf Larsen's personality: it produces interesting discussions but does not cause the events in the story. Larsen could have been the same sort of man without support from books; indeed, there is the background figure of his brother Death Larsen, who has 'all my brutishness, but he can scarcely read or write' and 'has never philosophised on life'.

Thrilling as the debates are, the personal implications remain those of a fantasy. Wolf Larsen is not immoral or objectionable as such a character would be in real life. He always commands the reader's sympathy, and ends as a tragic rather than a deservedly downfallen figure. In that sense there is no 'attack' at all. What is seen instead is Jack taking a hypothesis of individualism and making a superb drama; but to have done so did not affect the contradictions in his outlook. The question is recalled in *The Mutiny of the Elsinore*, which he wrote at the beginning of 1913. Primarily an adventure story, it is more unashamedly Nietzschean than *The Sea Wolf*. Jack had discovered and been temporarily stimulated by a manuscript called *Chameleon: Being the Book of My Selves,* by Benjamin De Casseres. He sent it to George Brett, and wrote: 'This man is really and truly the American Nietzsche. I, as you know, am in the opposite intellectual camp from that of Nietzsche. Yet no man in my own camp stirs me as does Nietzsche or as does De Casseres.'

Larsen's exciting character made *The Sea Wolf's* one flaw forgiveable. Most critics felt that its subsidiary theme, the love story of Humphrey Van Weyden and Maud Brewster, was thin-blooded to the point of absurdity. Ambrose Bierce wrote: 'I confess to an overwhelming contempt for both sexless lovers.'[28] This was due to the *Century* magazine more than to Jack. It was a relatively staid publication with a large family readership; enthusiastic as he was for the first half of *The Sea Wolf*, the editor, R.W.Gilder, noted that the synopsis for the remainder proposed to put the lovers alone on an island. His offer of four thousand dollars was subject to the magazine's right to alter and modify. Jack replied: 'He has my full permission to blue pencil all he wishes ... I am absolutely confident myself, that the American prudes will not be shocked by the last half of the book.' Though the lovers were drawn as respectable persons from the start, he was thus under notice to take care that they stayed so.

The short novel *The Game* was a product of one of his interests at this time, the boxing bouts at the West Oakland Athletic Club. It did not sell well, apparently on account of its subject-matter; curiously, it was more successful in Britain. He wrote several other boxing pieces in the same period. Unable to get in to the ringside places at the Club one evening, he was given a press seat by Fred Goodcell of the *Oakland Herald*. For a few months he regularly wrote short articles about the fights for the *Herald* in exchange for a ringside seat at each show. Later he was to be commissioned to describe world championship bouts for the Hearst press.

Jack's strongest impulse was always from immediate happenings. His philosophies and the declarations he made were constantly liable to be set aside for the excitement of the moment, or when he was roused by a book he had read. In January 1905 he began lecturing passionately on socialism again. One stimulus was the huge, unexpected vote for the Socialist Party's candidates in the elections of 1904 — Debs and Hanford polled almost half a million votes in their stand for the Presidency and Vice-Presidency of the United States, and in California alone over 35,000 voted for socialist candidates as against 7,575 in 1900. Another stimulus was the surging unrest in Russia. Everything Jack had said on his return from Japan was forgotten. He told the *San Francisco Examiner* that socialists in Japan and Russia alike were his comrades: 'For us socialists there are no boundaries, race, country or nationality.'

In January 1905, two days before Bloody Sunday in St Petersburg, he gave his lecture 'Revolution' at Berkeley University. A few days later he put his name with other radicals' to an appeal for funds to be sent to the Russian revolutionists. Still elated, he announced in a lecture to a businessmen's audience that the men who had killed Czarist officials were his brothers. In another speech he quoted William Lloyd Garrison's 'To hell with the Constitution', from a condemnation of slavery in 1856; others had used it, but Jack was generating so much excitement that newspaper headlines made the phrase his own.[29] The Oakland High School refused to allow him to lecture. In March he stood for

Mayor of Oakland but received only 981 votes. In April his *War of the Classes* was published; it was reprinted three times in the following seven months.

War of the Classes had been submitted to Macmillan in 1903. It was a collection of lectures and articles, which Brett had reservations about; in April 1904 Jack wrote from Korea asking him to give second thoughts to 'the expediency of not issuing as a book for an indefinitely long time to come'. The original title was 'The Salt of the Earth'. It was revised and renamed, and brought out quickly, on the strength of the apparent interest in socialism and the publicity Jack was receiving. There is no doubt that its publication was timely. In the wake of Jack's Berkeley lecture Upton Sinclair and some others had proposed the formation of the Intercollegiate Socialist Society. While support for the Socialist Party of America grew, the Industrial Workers of the World was founded to organise the great mass of the unskilled beneath a militant banner. Jack's special standing was not simply that he was a revolutionary who said daring things: he was the writer whom the workers read. His pieces were reproduced as five-cent pamphlets. In everyday American speech a 'Jack London socialist' meant one who would wage the class struggle without quarter.

Charmian had at last returned from Iowa and was living at Glen Ellen with her aunt. Until Jack's divorce was made final their relationship was kept concealed. His visits to Glen Ellen, accompanied by Manyoungi, were explained by Mrs Eames as retreats from his cares elsewhere. They corresponded, and Charmian went to his lectures and social gatherings. Not knowing how long they had to wait, she herself was uncertain where Jack's steps might lead while he was away from her. The press followed him expectantly, and his name was linked speculatively with various women — in February 1905 he wrote sardonically to Brett: 'I see you have not congratulated me upon my engagement to Blanche Bates. Why this cold unregard?'

A letter from Charmian to Jack shows what she feared:

> But the shock you gave me the night of your 'Scab' lecture in the city, made me very thoughtful. I saw you watch for her in the audience when you were through speaking; I saw you wave to her; I saw her backing and filling and fluttering after her manner. I saw you come together in the light of your

cigarette, and I knew that you had been together the evening before.

There is an affectation of light-heartedness in the letter — 'You're only a boy, after all, dear Man, and transparent enough'; but her heart must have been as heavy as lead. She and Ninetta Eames tried to persuade him to remain at Glen Ellen and work there, but he was disinclined; alternately restless and apathetic, he was unsure what he wanted to do. The turning point came in the middle of March. Jack had been cruising in the *Spray* along the rivers, accompanied some of the time by Cloudesley Johns. He discovered that he had a tumour. It was not malignant, but had been affecting him for some time and needed to be removed as soon as possible. After the operation, he is recorded as saying: 'I wonder how much of my intellectual 'Long Sickness' could have been traceable to this damned thing draining my system?'

Though the depressions which recurred throughout Jack's life were caused by psychological factors and drink, the tumour had been responsible for much of his low condition at this time. Free of it, he returned to Glen Ellen lively and enthusiastic, and responded to the beauties of the countryside. He had received $350 from the *Black Cat* for a story, and asked Charmian to buy him a horse with it. She chose carefully, a glorious chestnut-gold stallion named Washoe Ban, and rode it herself the twenty-two miles from San Francisco. She and Jack rode through the woods round Sonoma Mountain. He was beguiled by the name 'Valley of the Moon'; he joined in swimming and games with camping holidaymakers.

There was one special, superb view of hilly country covered with redwood trees, conifers and shrubs, in which an area of farmland had been cleared. When Jack learned that part of it was for sale, he rushed to buy it. Charmian had brought him there, shown him the view, hinted and praised; its realisation was vital for her. They made plans. They would hire a man to work for them, engage in every kind of farming, build a dream-house. The price of the land — a hundred and thirty acres in all — was $7000, and Jack agreed to buy horses, cows and farm machinery from the owner for another $600. He wrote to Brett asking for $10,000 against the *Sea Wolf* royalties, which were not due for some months.

Though Brett did not refuse, he disapproved. He spoke of the disadvantages in being tied to a venture in the country, 'no matter how beautiful and productive' (a reference to Jack's lyrical letter about the Sonoma redwoods and canyons). What was clearly in his mind was that in Jack he had a writer who would earn large sums of money and always live beyond them. A few months previously he had supplied an advance of $3000 to pay debts. He asked for interest to be paid on this latest and biggest advance, and suggested a new agreement from the end of the year, increasing the monthly payments to $300 and incorporating revised rates of royalties. His spirits must have sunk when he read the postscript to Jack's next letter: 'Oh, by the way, I've got another big project in view.'

After paying for the ranch Jack was nearly penniless. There was no more to come from Macmillan for a considerable time. His other liabilities rose steadily. In a letter at the beginning of October he mentioned insurance premiums of seven or eight hundred dollars; the monthly allowances to his mother and Bess; doctors' bills paid for relatives, and other undertakings given: 'And so on, & so on, and so on.' Personal desires for novelties and luxuries were taken for granted and seldom denied — shortly before the ranch project he had asked Brett for another advance to buy an automobile, but did not repeat the request. He told an interviewer from the *Examiner*: 'I'm always in debt.' The Korean house-boy Manyoungi pointed out where the light came between his fingers, and said it was where the hand leaked.

Jack spoke freely about his burdens, cataloguing them in letters to friends. He does not seem ever to have worried as most people would: rather, the debts were a measure of how far he had come in the world. The only protests he made were in dealings with Bess and, later, his daughter Joan; and they signify anger against the persons themselves and his compulsion to say that they hurt him all ways, including financially. To the rest of the world his stance was 'easy come, easy go'. In his short lifetime as a writer he was paid more than a million dollars, and practically every dollar was spoken for before it reached him. Charmian appears to have fallen in with his outlook, supporting every extravagant project; after his death she defended him as a good business man and dismissed critics as 'timid ones lacking his vision'.

Looking for more quick earnings, he thought of another dog story to follow the success of *The Call of the Wild*: 'Instead of the devolution or decivilisation of a dog, I'm going to give the evolution, the civilisation of a dog — development of domesticity, faithfulness, love, morality, and all the amenities and virtues.' This was *White Fang*. Assured of its certain success, Jack wrote it in two months; the serial rights, before Macmillan took it for book publication, were sold to the magazine *Outing* for $7,400. While he waited for the money, he arranged to go on an autumn lecture tour in the mid-west and the east under the management of the Slayton Lyceum Bureau. He was waiting for the news of his divorce. Charmian went to stay with her aunt at Newton, Iowa, and packed a trousseau in readiness for his call at any time.

The lecture tour began resoundingly. Jack lived up to his reputation and his publicity. He appeared as the handsome, virile young adventurer with a passion for social reform and a superb talent for words; he made a sensation. He spoke on his experiences as a hobo, in the Klondike, at sea, as a war correspondent, and his spectacular rise to literary renown. The speeches were not read from scripts as his earlier lectures had been; his soft voice and diffident manner reinforced the impression of a thoroughly romantic personality. One journalist wrote: 'He has been subjected to the same experiences as the matinee idol. However, he is without personal vanity.' In the cities he also gave speeches on socialism, having made a condition of the tour that he be left free to do so.

Then, on 18 November, in the fourth week of the tour, he received a telegram from California. The divorce was granted — he was free. He wired at once to Charmian. He was in Elyria, Ohio, and about to leave for Wisconsin. He would pass through Chicago: she must meet him there the next evening, and they would be married. She arrived and found Jack waiting without a marriage licence; it was Sunday, and the bureau was closed. There followed a series of scurries through the Chicago streets in a hansom cab to find an official who could marry them. He was asked why he could not wait until the morning, and insisted that he would not. Eventually a clerk was persuaded to go to the City Hall and open his office to make out a licence; the couple were directed to a Notary Public, J.J.Grant, who married them late at night in his home.

The newspapers were at Jack immediately. His lack of forethought is astonishing. He had told the Hearst press that a story concerning his personal life would break shortly, and promised them exclusive rights to it. He spoke to only the *Chicago*

American and turned the crowd of other reporters away; they responded by publishing derisive, censorious comments on his moral conduct. On Tuesday morning headlines alleged that his marriage to Charmian was invalid according to recent Illinois legislation. A judge refuted this, but the disapproval of this hasty marriage the day after the divorce remained (and was strengthened by Jack's own angry replies). As they continued the tour together, the change in the public's sentiment was shown unmistakably. A paper in Washington, Iowa, called Charmian 'the ugly-faced girl from California' and expressed the wish that she and Jack would go to sea and drown.

More seriously, women's clubs cancelled his lectures and one or two cities banned his books from their public libraries; and the radical press, his comrades, condemned him. His alleged immorality rebounded on them, enabling their opponents to cry that socialism meant sexual delinquency and the breaking-up of family life. Put on the defensive at a time when they were fighting to make a favourable impression, the radicals answered that Jack London's conduct had nothing to do with them and they disowned it. In this frame of mind they noted too Jack's taste for luxury: how he rode in Pullman coaches and was still attended by his servant. One accusation was that he had retarded the development of socialism by at least five years. Certainly he fell heavily in the esteem both of his readership and of his supporters. Three years later he wrote of 'a big slump in all my book-sales in the States', attributing it partly to general hard times and partly to his socialism; in fact it stemmed from the reaction to his second marriage.

The tour continued in more muted tones than it had begun. From Boston they went to Florida via the West Indies, then returned for Jack to address crowded meetings in New York and at Yale and Chicago universities. He delivered the 'Revolution' lecture and it was received enthusiastically on each occasion, but the newspapers were no longer friendly: he was described as 'a neurasthenic' and a 'socialistic sensation-monger'. There is one other view of him at that time, given by Upton Sinclair. As principal organiser for the Intercollegiate Socialist Society, Sinclair was present at the New York meeting and next day lunched with Jack and Charmian in Mouquin's restaurant together with the

editor of *Wilshire's* magazine. By his account in *The Cup of Fury,*
Jack was once more a heavy drinker.

> His eyelids were inflamed, and there were in his face and
> speech all the signs of alcoholism I had learned to recognise.
> He ordered drinks throughout the meal and during the hours
> of talk which followed.
> He chose to take my non-drinking as a challenge. Not in an
> angry way — and yet, as I look back with my present know-
> ledge of psychology, I know there must have been powerful
> conflicts in his subconscious. He chose to tease me by reciting
> his prodigious exploits as a drinking man.

The biographers' stories of Jack's drinking are all from his
own version in *John Barleycorn* and so go no further than the bouts
of his sailing days. Charmian's book says she never saw him tipsy.
While there are many references to his drinks, her claim is that
'upon him the effect of alcoholic stimulus was to render
preternaturally active an already superactive mind'. Sinclair says
he was a lifelong alcoholic: 'alcohol destroyed him'. It is hard to
imagine that the parties at his Piedmont home would have been so
boisterous without heavy drinking. Moreover, several of Jack's
'crowd' — George Sterling in particular — were excessive drinkers.
There is not much doubt that Sinclair's account is nearly enough
correct and Charmian's untrue and that a considerable amount of
Jack's erratic conduct, his depressions and outbursts, as well as his
ill-health, needs no other explanation.

The tour was cancelled after two or three more lectures.
Feeling 'miserably sick', he returned to Oakland with Charmian;
after he had bought a house for Flora, Johnny and Mammy Jenny
they went to Glen Ellen. Their home there was an annexe to Mrs
Eames's house, Wake Robin Lodge. While he supervised the work
of laying out their ranch, Jack applied himself to writing stories
and essays for the magazines and to make up collections for
Macmillan's to publish.

Despite its disturbed beginnings this year, 1906, became the
year of his greatest creative burst. He was writing to meet his need
for money: ready money from the magazines, and the building of
securities for further advances from Brett. He hunted for plots and
themes, any semblance of an idea for a marketable piece — indeed,

there were charges of plagiarism over the stories 'Love of Life' and 'The Unexpected', and *Before Adam*. [30] After he and Charmian had seen the effects of the San Francisco earthquake of 1906 Jack said no power on earth would make him write about it; but when *Collier's* offered him twenty-five cents a word, he did so.

The work he produced in these months was of his highest quality. The changes in his life — marriage, the new home, the interest provided by the ranch — seem to have given him fresh energy. Whatever its origins, 'Love of Life' is a gripping and superbly-written story. 'The Apostate' is another masterpiece. Besides other short stories there was Jack's vivid review, which the Hearst press censored, of Upton Sinclair's *The Jungle*: 'the 'Uncle Tom's Cabin' of Wage-Slavery'. And just before the end of the year he completed the book which by itself has given him lasting fame — *The Iron Heel*.

9. Turning: The Iron Heel

The removal to Glen Ellen marked a break in other ways. Jack's exhilaration over the prospects for socialism receded as quickly as it had risen. Nothing had followed the Socialist Party of America's electoral gains of 1904 — they represented only discontent with the oppressive growth of big business. Jack had ended his famous lecture with: 'The Revolution is here, now. Stop it who can.' He realised that the words had been hollow, and his other beliefs re-asserted themselves. At the same time, resentments had grown between him and his comrades. They had criticised him, and he did not like opposition; he began to speak of the time and effort he had given, and conjectural losses from it. He wrote to Sterling:

> I feel that I have done and am doing a pretty fair share of work for the Revolution. I guess my lectures alone before socialist organisations have netted the Cause a few hundred dollars, and my wounded feelings from the personal abuse of the Capitalist papers ought to be rated at several hundred more ... The amount of work that I in a year contribute to the cause of socialism would earn me a whole lot of money if spent in writing fiction for the market.[31]

There was no question of his severing connections with the Socialist Party, and he continued giving money to help it. However, there is every sign that his circle of friends now began in the main to reflect the successful writer, and socialists had only a minor place in it; and that this was of his and Charmian's choosing.

Other elements came into the re-formation of his social life. Many of his friends had disapproved of his conduct with Charmian, in particular because they had concealed their relationship. In the autumn of 1905 Jack wrote two long, angry letters to George Sterling's wife Carrie, who had reproached him on several people's behalf. 'For weeks past', he wrote, 'the gossip has been dribbling back that the Crowd dropped Charmian because Charmian broke up the London family.' 'The Crowd' virtually ceased to exist, and the feelings of blame and disparagement for Charmian remained throughout their lives. Another factor was Jack's insistence, amounting almost to a mania, on always being seen to be right. His friends were required to be acolytes, making only the responses which fed his opinion of himself.

For that reason the socialists for whom he expressed high admiration were, in practice, at a distance. George Speed, whom he first met in Kelly's Army and who came nearest to his ideal of the class-conscious, uncompromising proletarian, was a San Francisco man; Jack esteemed him but never made him a friend. Similarly, he kept apart from such people as Austin Lewis and Jane Roulston. The latter, a woman of remarkable character, appeared in *The Iron Heel* as Anna Roylston, the Red Virgin. She and Lewis had been close observers and critics of the younger Jack; neither of them would have been tolerant to his subsequent outlook. A friendship with Ernest Untermann was sustained on conditions of which Untermann eventually complained, in Jack's words:

> ... you say that it is a pity that you were broke when I first met you, and when you say that this state of being broke placed you in a very disadvantageous position for real friendship right at the start, and when you say that this condition of being broke gave you a feeling that Charmian never quite outgrew the fear that you were trying to take unfair advantage of my generosity.[32]

Charmian gives a list of some of the visitors to Glen Ellen in 1906. They were mostly artists and literary and professional people; one or two, like George Wharton James and Professor Bland, published agreeable articles about the Londons. Jack went frequently to the Bohemian Club in San Francisco, where he and George Sterling and Jimmy Hopper were members. His closest friendship undoubtedly was with Sterling. It was a curious, heavily emotional relationship. Sterling was several years older than Jack, one of the numerous minor poets of the Bay area. The two men had known each other since 1900; their friendship expanded in the Piedmont days, but became a blaze after Jack's return from Japan in 1904. Sterling called him 'Wolf', probably at Jack's own request — from the same period he signed his letters to Cloudesley Johns also as 'Wolf'. His name for Sterling was 'Greek', a reference to the poet's profile.

The correspondence between them contains open expressions of affection. Jack's letters begin with such phrases as 'Dearest Greek' and 'Blessed Greek'. Probably these became merely habitual over the years, but they plainly had conscious meaning in 1905. One letter from Jack ends:

> No, I am afraid the dream was too bright to last — our being near to each other. If you don't understand now, someday sooner or later you may come to understand. It's not through any fault of yours, nor through any fault of mine. The world and people just happen to be so made.

It is possible to see this partly as talk from an intellectual vogue, imitating the poses of the aesthetic movement in England. Sterling made that kind of bohemianism his style. He had been intended for the priesthood; now, when away from his white-collar job, he affected social and moral unconventionality. But neither man was innocent of the implications of their words. For Jack they were the voice of his longing for the 'Man-Comrade' in whom so many dreams were vested.

One other potent influence on Jack's life at this time was Charmian's aunt, Mrs Eames. The *Overland Monthly* had closed down; she and Edward Payne had been responsible for building Wake Robin Lodge and the cabins she rented out. Ninetta's part in the relationship between Jack and Charmian had always been a pushing, supervisory one. To have them now beside her, with this celebrated young man as her virtual son-in-law, went to her head. She took charge in every way possible, intruding and demanding. Two weeks before their marriage Jack wrote to Charmian, from New York: 'What does Aunt Netta mean by saying 'all her moments' 'are given to the work Jack set' her? I don't understand. Forwarding mail — yes. Keeping mice out of my clothes — yes. But what else?' In a short time, however, he was accepting her as their major-domo and consenting to her self-appointment as his secretary. He was drawn too into association with Mrs Eames's companion, Payne. He was a former preacher who dabbled in spiritualism; though Jack called him a 'Metaphysician', without much doubt he was a charlatan. Ninetta had been won over to spiritualism, and Jack was pressed — until he rebelled — into frequent discussions with Payne, who apparently hoped for Jack's conversion.

There was a further project in 1906 which emphasised his wish to break away from former surroundings and interests. Full as the year was, Jack plunged into work on the *Snark*, the boat on which he and Charmian proposed to sail round the world. The idea had been born at Glen Ellen the previous year, in the weeks when they were excitedly buying the ranch. By all their accounts it arose from reading Joshua Slocum's book about his own three years' voyage;[33] and was abetted by Roscoe Eames, Ninetta's sixty-year-old husband, who was a seasoned yachtsman and eager for such a venture. They would do it, they said, when the ranch was in order and their house was built: perhaps in four or five years' time. But waiting was not in Jack's nature, and in a few days he and Charmian had decided the time must be now. He wrote:

> The ultimate word is I LIKE. It lies beneath philosophy, and is twined about the heart of life. When philosophy has maundered ponderously for a month, telling the individual what he must do, the individual says in an instant, 'I LIKE', and does something else, and philosophy goes glimmering. It is I LIKE that makes the drunkard drink and the martyr wear a hair shirt ... Philosophy is very often a man's way of explaining his own I LIKE.[34]

It was firmly in his mind that the boat must be his own in every way. There was no shortage of sea-going boats for sale, but this would be made to Jack's specification. He read everything he could on boat-building and engines, and put Roscoe in charge of carrying out his plans with the instruction: 'Spare no money. Let everything on the *Snark* be of the best.' The original estimate for building and fitting was seven thousand dollars; in fact by the time the *Snark* left in April 1907 it had cost thirty thousand. Some of the delays were due to the San Francisco earthquake and fire. Workshops, factories and stocks had been destroyed and labour was scarce.

Orders had to be sent to New York; repeatedly, nothing was done for weeks on end. But costly ineptitude abounded. Would-be sailors and workmen of little competence joined the payroll. Useless materials were bought, and essential ones not delivered. The reckless spending gave rise to a story that the whole thing was backed by a rich magazine; prices soared when the *Snark* was mentioned.

Jack drove on through the chaos. His plan had been to finance the construction with advances from magazines against contracts to write for them during the voyage. As soon as he and Charmian made their decision, in February 1906, he wrote to the *Cosmopolitan, McClure's, Collier's* and *Outing*. His letter began dramatically: 'The keel is laid' (that did not happen until four months later). It went on to describe what the boat would be like and give a detailed itinerary of its world cruise. Reminding them of his reputation as a story-teller and reporter, Jack made his proposition and asked each editor for three thousand dollars in advance. There would be no duplication of material, and on that condition the magazines were willing enough. Bailey Millard, the editor of the *Cosmopolitan*, showed high enthusiasm for the idea: he wanted the boat named after his magazine, and suggested that other well-known writers be brought in to send letters to Jack during the voyage. However, as time went by Millard began to be sceptical that the *Snark* would ever sail, and Jack's buoyant letters to him were replaced by acrimonious ones. There were quarrels with other editors as he turned out and pressed upon them everything he could, determined that 'I like' should not be denied.

The *Snark* was nowhere near completion by October, the projected sailing date. It had consumed twelve thousand dollars in eight months. White-bearded Roscoe Eames was a calamity in himself, creating further disorganisation at every turn. He believed the journey would be made inside the earth, which he claimed to be a hollow sphere. Jack sent him home with an ultimatum to revise his views and study navigation. Taking out mortgages on the ranch and Flora's house, Jack hired fourteen workmen and paid them an extra dollar a day for working fast. New dates were announced — November, December, January. The newspapers were now treating the matter with derision, and cuttings arrived from England revealing that it had become a joke there too. They quoted

Jack's flamboyant early announcement that 'no writer of prominence' had sailed round the world: nor, it seemed, would he. Sailing experts asserted that the boat was an incompetent botch and would founder if ever it put to sea. Jack's friends made bets about its future.

Angrily, he decided to sail the vessel as it was to Honolulu and have the building finished there. He borrowed a further five thousand dollars from a bank: misfortunes consumed it at once. First there was a leak and then, en route to the boatways, the *Snark* was crushed between two barges. It stood on its stern in the mud while tugs waited for the tides. An attempt to use the windlass, for which power was to come from the engine, showed defective castings; the gears ground together, and windlass and engine were both shattered. The work began again. At last in April, still leaking and problem-ridden, it was deemed ready to start. A crowd assembled on the Oakland wharf, and another crowd on board. At the last moment a bailiff came and tacked a notice on the mast: an attachment granted to a creditor, forbidding the *Snark* to move until $232 was paid. The departure did not take place until two days later.

Despite all the crises and 'inconceivable and monstrous' events which haunted and protracted the construction, Jack went on writing and making plans for his ranch. A month after leaving he applied to Brett for another advance — he had already had six thousand dollars and wanted another five thousand. In the letter he said: 'You see, hand in hand with the building of the *Snark*, I have gone on with the building of the ranch in Glen Ellen. I have a magnificent barn on it, all paid for, and also thousands of dollars worth of improvements in the way of orchard, vineyard, wild trees (that I planted), fences, etc.' He wrote tirelessly, frequently at night-time: he and Charmian had separate bedrooms because he spent the nights 'reading, writing, smoking and coughing'. In the summer, when the *Snark*'s keel was laid, he started work on *The Iron Heel*. It is one of his longest books, and the writing cannot have been easy; yet the finished manuscript was despatched to Macmillan's on 13 December.

The Iron Heel is commonly assessed as a prophetic work, and the common assumptions are that it expounds Jack London's socialist convictions and shows the depth of his reading of socialist philosophy. All three are mistaken. The idea that it set out to predict events was one he himself denied. Charmian — who has very little to say about *The Iron Heel* — records him saying to her: 'I *didn't* write the thing as a prophecy at all.' In the copy he gave her he wrote: 'we that have seen what we've seen — we may not see these particular things come to pass, but certain it is that we shall see big things of some sort come to pass.' To Brett, in his letter following the manuscript, he said: 'Personally, I think from a pseudo-scientific standpoint the situation of *The Iron Heel* is plausible.'

The prophetic claim was made by Anatole France in his preface to the first French edition in 1924, after Mussolini's rise to power in Italy. It was repeated by Trotsky in 1937 — 'The fact is incontestable: in 1907 Jack London already foresaw and described the fascist régime as the inevitable result of the defeat of the proletarian revolution.'[35] It is understandable why they and others, including Orwell, should have found *The Iron Heel* apposite to the development of fascism in Europe in the nineteen-twenties and -thirties. However, there is little in the book to carry the comparison far, other than its conception of violent repression. Had it been possible for Jack to be conscious of fascism as a political creed, he might have found an affinity with it in the faith he stated to Johns in 1899, in which socialism was declared to be only an instrument for giving 'more strength to these certain kindred races so that they may survive and inherit the earth to the extinction of the weaker, lesser races'. This was not the outcome of the defeat of the proletarian revolution but, for Jack, the reason why the revolution would not happen.

The fact is that Jack's period as a socialist was over. He found no need to disavow it, or to cease his associations formally. It was a part of his reputation that he did not wish to renounce, any more than he relinquished being an authority on social questions. Nevertheless, he had parted ways with the idea of a mass working-class movement to overthrow capitalism and establish a new society. His enthusiasm for it had always been sporadic, shadowed by conflicting beliefs and rising over them only when there was some special stimulus. The lecturing and headline-making of 1905 were its last surge. It was to be followed by loss of interest, deprecation and near-contempt. The socialists, by criticising him, confirmed his conviction that they were weaklings who would fail. If they tried their revolution they would be crushed as the Russian rebels had been, and the honourable exceptions among them would be martyrs.

The socialists themselves were aware that he had dropped the Cause and was about to leave the scene indefinitely. They addressed reproachful statements on the *Snark*'s departure as to a lost leader. It was indeed a symbolic farewell, and *The Iron Heel* was part of Jack's preparation for it. There might have been more to it: his persistence that the *Snark* must go to sea whatever the cost may be seen as a desperate attempt to break away. The alternative was to remain, not only with personal associations, but to be confronted by a dilemma — he admired the intellectual qualities of socialism but knew for certain now that he did not accept it.

The Iron Heel's reputation as a socialist classic derives from its first half, in which the case against capitalism is expounded dramatically. The upholders of the system are discredited and exposed in debate with the hero, Ernest Everhard. This part of the book culminates in a speech to an audience of the wealthiest members of society — the master class; he flays and enrages them, and returns their challenge with his own.

> Power, you have proclaimed the king of words. Very good. Power it shall be. And in the day that we sweep to victory at the ballot-box, and you refuse to turn over to us the government we have constitutionally and peacefully captured, and you demand what we are going to do about it — in that day, I say, we shall answer you; and in roar of shell and shrapnel and in whine of machine-guns shall our answer be couched.

Everhard is presented as a paragon of physical strength, learning, foresight and bravery. He is, as Joan London wrote, 'the revolutionist Jack would have liked to be if he had not, unfortunately, also desired to be several other kinds of men'. There is a strong personal fantasy in all these early chapters. Everhard's opponents in argument — metaphysicians, business men, lawyers — supply openings for the crushing answers and expositions he has at the ready. It is likely that the fantasy has worked for readers too. As George Orwell wrote: 'the kind of book which consists of conversations where the person whom the author agrees with has the best of it is quite obviously a way of revenging the conversational defeats which one suffers in real life'.[36]

The debates show the deficiencies of Jack's understanding of socialism very clearly. His presentation of its economics, Marx's theory of value, takes place in a chapter named 'The Mathematics of a Dream'. Everhard promises his hearers at the outset: 'I shall develop the inevitability of the breakdown of the capitalist system, and I shall demonstrate mathematically why it must break down.' As the argument progresses Jack's old perplexity of 'The Question of the Maximum' is revealed. The nature of capitalist production, and the surplus value produced in each working day, is explained in simple outline: but what happens then?

> The United States is a capitalist country that has developed its resources. According to its capitalist system of industry, it has an unconsumed surplus that must be got rid of, and that must be got rid of abroad. What is true of the United States is true of every other capitalist country with developed resources. Every one of such countries has an unconsumed surplus ... Now, gentlemen, follow me. The planet is only so large. There are only so many countries in the world. What will happen when every country in the world, down to the smallest and last, with a surplus on its hands, stands confronting every other country with surpluses on their hands?

Much of Marx's work was still not available in English in 1906. Only the first volume of *Capital* had been translated; Jack could not have been aware of 'the theory of the law of the falling tendency of the rate of profit' in the third volume, on which predictions of the breakdown of capitalism were later to be based. His argument was a familiar one in the early years of the socialist movement: that the crises of capitalism arose from the fact of more wealth being produced than the working class — or the capitalists themselves — could buy back. Nevertheless, more sophisticated Marxists were able to see its fallacy. If this were the whole truth, there could never be a trade boom, and crisis would be continuous.

From this insurmountable difficulty of the capitalist system, Jack advances to his statement of the alternatives. One is socialism, the seizure of the surplus-producing machines by labour to found 'a new and tremendous era'. The other is the defeat of labour by the combined force of the trusts: 'a despotism as relentless and terrible as any despotism that has blackened the pages of the history of man'. Moreover, this 'Oligarchy' has its own means for disposing of the surpluses.

> Magnificent roads will be built. There will be great achievements in science, and especially in art ... It will be great art, I tell you, and wonder cities will arise that will make tawdry and cheap the cities of old time. And in these cities will the oligarchs dwell and worship beauty.
>
> Thus will the surplus be constantly expended while labor does the work. The building of these great works will give a starvation ration to millions of common laborers, for the enormous bulk of the surplus will compel an equally enormous expenditure, and the oligarchs will build for a thousand years — ay, for ten thousand years. They will build as the Egyptians and the Babylonians never dreamed of building; and when the oligarchs have passed away, their great roads and their wonder cities will remain for the brotherhood of labor to tread upon and dwell within.

The Oligarchy does indeed triumph. Everhard loses his life, and the socialist movement is reduced to remnants either dispirited or carrying out revengeful terrorism.

All this superimposes other theories on a scarcely rendered Marxism. The theory of value is used not as Marx formulated it, as the detailed working-out of the class struggle in twentieth-century industrial society, but merely to show the dilemma of the capitalist class. With the rise of the Oligarchy, Marx's theory appears to be no longer applicable. Instead, two theories are made operative that between them maintain political and economic stability for the ruling class. The first is identified in the book as that put forward by W.J.Ghent in 1902, in *Our Benevolent Feudalism*: 'It has always been insisted that Ghent put the idea of the Oligarchy into the minds of the great capitalists.' The second is General Coxey's 'roads' scheme.

Ghent's book had made a deep impression on Jack. Its thesis was that from the visible growth of huge monopolies in American industry there would come a single colossus in which all capital was integrated: 'a gigantic merger of all interests, governed by a council of ten'. This was a modern feudalism, far more complex than the economic order of the Middle Ages but 'based upon the same status of lord, agent and underling'. Ghent may have used the word 'benevolent' ironically, but Jack's imagination was roused by the vision of such a dictatorship. He saw the Oligarchy as a collective superman standing astride the civilised world. Theoretically labour was stronger by weight of numbers; but the oligarchs were disciplined and intelligent as the majority of labour were not. In *The Iron Heel* one reason for labour's defeat is the other leaders' failure to grasp the truths which Everhard points out.

The Oligarchy's economics reveal that the idea of public works as a cure-all had lain in Jack's mind since 1894. It is unmistakably Coxey, beginning with 'magnificent roads' and producing a new pyramid age in which hordes are kept employed and economic problems disposed of as successfully as they would be by socialism. One may wonder why Jack had not advocated this solution before. The answer is that he identified it with socialism — it is implicit, for instance, in his essay 'What Communities Lose by the Competitive System'. It required an immense centralisation of society, of which he thought capitalism incapable until he read Ghent's book. It is significant that the essay, written in 1899, said the centralisation would necessarily involve a loss of liberty:

> Internal competition must be minimised and industry yield more and more to the co-operative principle. For the good of the present and future generations, certain rights of the individual must be curtailed or surrendered. Yet this is nothing new to the individual; his whole past is a history of such surrenders.

Without doubt *The Iron Heel* contains a trenchant indictment of capitalist society, of its 'pig-ethics' and some types of its upholders. That this order of things should be replaced, Jack was sure. But the book is also his statement of why socialism was not achievable in the foreseeable future. It required leaders full of courage and prescience, and followers such as they deserved; with rare exceptions, neither existed. The ending shows all too clearly Jack's rejection of the idea that the working-class mass had the capacity to help itself. 'The people of the abyss' are re-created in this final episode of the Chicago Commune. They are shown as degraded and irresponsible, 'content with misery'; let loose, they are a mob without a purpose other than destruction.

The struggle depicted in *The Iron Heel* is the Darwinian one, for supremacy by the strongest. That is not inconsonant with a socialist view: classes rise, overthrow older classes and establish new social orders because they *are* stronger and socially fitter. However, Jack placed the conflict in the setting of personal capacity for power. Everhard is 'a superman, a blond beast such as Nietzsche described', and fit to rule the world. But the oligarchs are stronger still, and he is let down by his comrades and the masses; his defeat is inevitable. It is true that socialism eventually comes to pass — the book is presented as from the distant future — but in a manner which gives no credit to the socialist movement. The Oligarchy is not overcome in any struggle. After several centuries it is weakened by in-breeding among its privileged castes; there are palace revolutions, so that 'in the end the common people ... come into their own'. This downfall is reminiscent, in fact, of Wolf Larsen's. The counter-forces could not triumph on their own; they are helped by an extra factor.

The message is of Jack's loss of faith. He would have said (as others have) that he was disillusioned. He had thrust out vivid, urgent expectations which were indeed beyond the radical movement and the working class; and certainly the leaders of the American left quickly followed their European counterparts on the paths of reform and compromise. Nevertheless, his socialism had self-deception in it from the start. The pleasures of intellectual company, of being lionised, of always having a platform waiting, caused him to set aside or rationalise the differences which were plainly there. When his expectations were douched and the 'I like' of his personal life opposed, he uttered what he had always believed above all: that the strong would rule the weak.

He considered that the spread of interest in socialism would make *The Iron Heel* sell, though it was not magazine material; as he expected, Brett took it for Macmillan. It was published while he was on the *Snark* in the Pacific Ocean. Possibly he intended to be away from the scene when its impressions were created. Its reception by the press was not good. The newspapers and magazines were indifferent, giving only meagre notices or none at all. The radical press attacked it for its pessimism and its preoccupation with violence. In the *International Socialist Review* John Spargo called it 'an unfortunate book'.

> The picture he gives is well calculated, it seems to me, to repel many of those whose addition to our forces is sorely needed; it gives a new impetus to the old and generally discarded cataclysmic theory; it tends to weaken the political Socialist movement and to encourage the chimerical and reactionary notion of physical force, so alluring to a certain type of mind ...

B.O.Flower's left-wing magazine *Arena* said the book showed a misreading of history, and was 'a detriment rather than a help to the cause of social justice'. Those who found in its favour were chiefly the activists. For them, what mattered were the propagandist chapters; the rest was unimportant speculation. But those who might have commented best — Austin Lewis, Untermann, Anna Strunsky — were silent. They knew *The Iron Heel*'s true meaning.

Its fame and the growth of a world-wide readership came after the first world war, when Jack was dead. Then, the naked power used by the ruling class against communism brought his picture to life. It was the only American book named by Bukharin in a bibliography of works on communism. George Orwell, in a preface written in 1945, claimed mistakenly that it was brought out of obscurity by Hitler's coming to power.[37] This error gives the key to why *The Iron Heel* is continually discovered by fresh generations; like Orwell's own *Nineteen Eighty-Four*, it contains much which on the surface is apparently true at any time.

10. The Snark Voyage

The *Snark*'s voyage went on for more than two years. It appears as a saga of folly and misfortune, ending in a debt-laden return; yet Jack was happy. Though he quarrelled and laid about him, sent furious haranguing letters, hired and fired among his crew, a curious elatedness ran through it all. He wrote prolifically, setting himself a minimum of a thousand words a day and seldom failing to do it. During the two years he produced five books, and the equivalent of two or three more in articles and short stories. Charmian also wrote. She had undertaken to keep a descriptive diary of the voyage: the outcome was two books which Macmillan published (produced as four separate titles in Britain — *Voyaging in Wild Seas, A Woman among the Head Hunters, Jack London in Hawaii* and *Jack London in Southern Seas*).

The months they spent in the South Sea Islands furnished new material for Jack. He was thrilled by the scenery and the views of primitive life. From the Solomons he wrote to Sterling: 'This is about the rawest edge of the world. Head-hunting, cannibalism and murder are rampant. Among the worst islands of the group, day and night we are never unarmed, and night watches are necessary.' He made the South Seas his new Yukon, where adventures and drama were enacted in a spate of stories — even, later, a pair of dog stories. Sitting on the deck on warm afternoons he read to Charmian and the crew: sometimes from his own morning's work, at other times from Conrad, Melville and Robert Louis Stevenson.

Six weeks after they set out, he finally dismissed Roscoe Eames in Pearl Harbour. The decks had not been washed for twelve days; the masts and sails were untouched; Roscoe would hardly lift a finger in whatever situation. Almost certainly there were concealed reasons for this grotesque, inadequate man's presence on the *Snark*. When Jack refused to tolerate him any more, Mrs Eames sent a cable in code asking him 'to with-hold pillorying Roscoe' until she and Edward Payne gave a clearance for doing so. Jack wrote her a long letter detailing the offences and negligences, and said: 'For the first time I really appreciate what you have endured. And I cannot help calling you a silly, sentimental fool for having endured it for so long, as you have.' Not long afterwards Ninetta divorced Roscoe and married Payne.

Herbert Stolz was fired on Roscoe's heels. His place was taken by Eugene Fenelon, a muscular giant recommended by George Sterling. In a few weeks he too was sent back to California, and Jack was writing to Sterling: 'Gene was not made for adventure, nor was he made for manhood ... With the body of a primitive, of a gorilla, he has the guts of a louse and the soul of a chicken!' When the *Snark* left Hilo its crew comprised Captain Warren, a paroled murderer; Martin Johnson; Frank Herman; an oriental cook named Wada; and the Londons' houseboy Nakata (Manyoungi had fallen out with Jack before the voyage began). Warren was engaged when Jack acknowledged at last that he needed an experienced sea-captain. The two who stood out above everyone, however, were Martin Johnson and Charmian. Johnson later became famous as an explorer and big-game hunter; now, a good-looking young man who wanted adventure, he turned his hand to every need on the *Snark*. Charmian worked like a man. She wrote her diary, typed Jack's manuscripts and his letters, stood day and night watches at the wheel, and did a generous share of all the boat's chores.

From Hawaii they sailed for the Marquesas Islands. Recalling his feats with Young Scratch and how he had shot the White Horse rapids, Jack wanted to take the hardest routes everywhere. 'The *South Sea Directory* says that the whaleship captains doubted if it could be accomplished from Hawaii to Tahiti — which is much easier than to the Marquesas', he wrote. The journey took sixty days. Its rewards were to see the haunts of R.L.S. and the ruins of the beautiful valley of Melville's *Typee*, and to take in the native dances and festivals. Jack had to go to Australia, where he reported the world heavyweight championship fight between Tommy Burns and Jack Johnson for the *New York Herald*. Then they set sail for

Tahiti — where at Papeete, in January 1908, three months' mail awaited them. They learned that the *Snark* had been feared lost, the newspapers uncertain whether to prepare obituaries or to discover that it was a publicity stunt.

There was much worse news. Jack's finances had reached a crisis. His cheques were being returned by the Oakland bank; the mortgage on Flora's house had been foreclosed; and bills were still pouring in. There were cheques for royalties from Brett in the Papeete pile, but other expected payments had not come. On a swift calculation Jack possessed only $66 against liabilities which were almost gigantic, and the *Snark* was costing $3000 a month to sail. Some action had to be taken. He and Charmian left the *Snark* in Captain Warren's hands, and headed for San Francisco on the steamer *Mariposa*, with a return to Papeete eight days after landing.

Ninetta Eames had been left in charge of Jack's affairs, but could not be blamed for a situation which had been developing since 1903. In four and a half years he had spent nearly a hundred thousand dollars on the ranch and the *Snark*, Bess's house and Flora's house, and his real or acquired dependents. The greater part of the money was used in advance of being earned, creating a treadmill which required a near-superhuman effort to work. Yet the only solution now was to ask for a further advance. As soon as he was in San Francisco Jack cabled Macmillan for funds against the novel he had nearly completed, *Martin Eden*. He contacted *Harper's Magazine* and arranged publication — for immediate payment — of articles about the *Snark*. Enough was raised to pay the most pressing debts. This done, he confirmed Ninetta's standing as his agent, with authority to raise loans on his behalf. In his letters he now addressed her as 'Mother Mine'. She in turn asked for $30 a month, and a commission on the sale of *Martin Eden*. He wrote: 'One of the things I have prided myself on since I have had a dollar to spend, has been that everybody that ever did anything for me has always been well paid.'

With the crisis met for the time being, he and Charmian returned to the *Snark*. The seven years' voyage was still on, and their blithe mood unchanged. Jack told the newspapermen in San Francisco that he was happier than he had ever been in his life; one journalist wrote of 'The smile that won't come off'. On the

Mariposa and back in Papeete he finished *Martin Eden* and mailed it to Ninetta; the sale of the serial rights to the *Pacific Monthly* for $7000 brought solvency again. Jack bought curios and souvenirs in huge quantities, and sent them in box after box to Glen Ellen to be unpacked and stored. Even the tropical ailments which affected everyone on the *Snark* were treated light-heartedly: 'One is in absolute harmony with Nature's laws when a yellow-fever mosquito bites.'

The elation came largely from the sense of being at the head of a historic adventure. It was also the product of the mental independence for which the *Snark* stood. Jack turned away from socialism and made a wider repudiation, of the world in which he existed during his rise from obscurity to fame — the questing relationships and mistaken idealisations, the struggle for personal as well as literary acceptance. He did not aim to deny his earlier years of reckless and disreputable adventures and hard work; indeed, they formed a background of which he was always proud. But he had to expunge the gauche young man with his feelings of mental inferiority and his political naiveté, the young man who had blurted out his hopes and frustrations to Mabel Applegarth. In sailing away, he celebrated his escape from the sights and associations of that self. In *Martin Eden* he re-wrote his life.

It was preceded by *The Road*, in which he told fully of his times as a hobo. A few years previously he had shied away from producing such a book, with its stories of low life and prison. Now he proclaimed the experiences triumphantly. Replying to a critical reviewer, he said: 'I have become what I am because of my past; and if I am ashamed of my past, logically I must be ashamed of what that past made me become.' He reproached Sterling, who voiced objections, with having 'a lingering taint of the bourgeois'. Undoubtedly *The Road* shocked many people when it appeared in 1907, but in Jack's *Snark* mood that was to the good. The 'I' who wrote it was the self whose existence he recognised, and *Martin Eden* was the continuation of that self as he wished it to be.

Jack told Martin Johnson he had used his name for the book's hero. Its original title was 'Success'. It is scarcely disguised autobiography. Martin Eden, the virile and uneducated young sailor with a burning desire to learn and to write, is introduced to the middle-class home of the Morse family. He falls in love with the delicate, beautiful Ruth Morse; she is drawn to him and becomes his tutor. He spends a year working for success as a writer, going without food and sleep, turning out masses of stories. Ruth is repelled by the realism of his writing; he offends her family by asserting a materialist philosophy; none of them believes in his ability to succeed. Ruth breaks off their engagement just before success comes. She returns penitently to him, but he rejects her contemptuously.

It is difficult to conceive that these were living persons, and that the principal one was the girl Jack had loved less than ten years before. Ruth Morse was Mabel Applegarth, to the point of physical resemblance. Some of the conversations in the book had taken place between them. The background was the Applegarths' home, and Mrs Morse was Mabel's mother. They and her brother Ted — Jack's friend and confidant — were shown as small-minded, ignorant and despicable. According to Irving Stone, a lecturer to the San José Women's Club in 1910 condemned the heroine of *Martin Eden* without knowing 'that the pale, ethereal, spinsterish-looking woman in the front row, gazing up at her with death in her eyes' was Mabel. In many ways *Martin Eden* is one of the most spiteful books ever written, arraigning people to whom Jack in fact owed something in his development.

Yet this was part of the motif. Martin Eden, like Jack, owed nobody. His talent is not fostered but is there all the time seeking recognition: to prove the point, when he has become famous he sends back to editors his early rejected manuscripts and sees them received eagerly.

> Why didn't you give me a dinner then? It was work performed. If you are feeding me now for work performed, why did you not feed me then when I needed it? Not one word of 'The Ring of Bells', nor of 'The Peri and the Pearl' has been changed. No; you're not feeding me now for work performed. You are feeding me because everybody else is feeding me and because it is an honour to feed me.'

As a reflection on social values and the meretriciousness of fashionable acclaim, that is true enough (though the claim 'work performed' is seductive when made with hindsight from the viewpoint of success). But a more fundamental statement is being made. So far from contributing a phase to his development, Mabel and her family and friends had only obstructed his drive to success.

All this was thought out in the summer before the *Snark* sailed: a season of turning, of viewing a future filled with 'I like' and of rejecting whatever there was from the past to fetter him. Once the rationalisation was decided upon, the angry scorn was characteristically Jack. But *Martin Eden's* vindictiveness is more than that; one senses that Mabel had remained too strongly in his mind. After *Martin Eden* he wrote from Tahiti to Cloudesley Johns: 'Have just finished a 145,000 word novel that is an attack upon the bourgeoisie and all that the bourgeoisie stands for.' That was an exaggeration. His condemnation was of the comfortable, culturally pretentious middle class. He had to purge himself of the disagreeable knowledge that he had aspired to their kind of life. It was found not only in the Applegarth circle, but among the socialists of Oakland, in the Strunskys' home, and in his own marriage to Bess; they belonged to a past of which he now washed his hands.

The other element in *Martin Eden* is a political one. Like Jack, Martin attends socialist meetings. He debates the subject with Russ Brissenden, whose personality and flow of philosophical knowledge make a picture of Strawn-Hamilton. Despite Brissenden's arguments, Martin cannot accept socialism; he is an individualist, steeped in Spencer and Nietzsche. This is made the eventual focus of the book. Disillusioned by success and having nothing to hold him to life, Martin drowns himself. Brissenden has warned him: 'I'd like to see you a socialist before I'm gone. It will give you a sanction for your existence. It is the one thing that will save you in the time of your disappointment that is coming to you.' The implication, to which Jack drew attention several times, is that for the individualist the outlook is hopeless.

However, the alternative for Martin is little different. The socialists appear as erudite weaklings, typifying 'the age-long struggle of the feeble, wretched slaves against the lordly handful of men who had ruled over them and would rule over them'. Brissenden himself is a cynic without faith in the masses. He is a socialist only because it is 'inevitable' in an unexplained way; and he, like Martin, dies. Jack had decided that neither outlook offered fulfilment for society or self. Intellectually he recognised socialism as the rational alternative to the present system, on the understanding that to work for it was futile. Emotionally he knew himself to be an individualist, but knew also that individualism was untenable. No creed could claim him now; for the future, he was his own man.

There is one other aspect of *Martin Eden* to be noted. It was the last work in which he strove for the 'worth-while' in content. From the beginning of his career he had never concealed that he wrote primarily for money. Nevertheless, he had presented his outlook in his stories, and he had come to believe that he could expound important truths in commercially successful books. The last three, differing widely as individual works, all dramatised the reassessment he was making of his life and beliefs. All — *The Iron Heel, The Road* and *Martin Eden* — were received unfavourably. The reviewers perceived his introspection, and expressed the wish that he would go back to uncomplicated story-telling. This provided the final confirmation of the view he now took of himself. It is, indeed, stated in *Martin Eden*:

> It was the bourgeoisie who bought his books and poured its gold into his money-sack, and from what little he knew of the bourgeoisie it was not clear to him how it could possibly appreciate or comprehend what he had written. His intrinsic beauty and power meant nothing to the hundreds of thousands who were acclaiming him and buying his books. He was the fad of the hour, the adventurer who had stormed Parnassus while the gods nodded.

Again, this was untrue; but it represented what Jack had resolved about his writing in future. He was finished with serious work, and would turn out adventure stories like cheap china for the highest profits. His next novel, *Burning Daylight*, returned to the Klondike. To an interviewer in 1911 he said: 'If it's good, I sign it and send it out. If it isn't good, I sign it and send it out.'

When the *Snark*'s voyage was resumed it took them to Polynesia, thence through storms to the Fiji Islands. At Suva Captain Warren, who had shown himself subject to violent depressive fits, either left or was dismissed and Jack took charge. They cruised on to the Solomons; there were escapes from cannibals, and a 'black-birding' expedition — hunting bushmen to carry them away to be slaves in the plantations. The novel *Adventure* that came out of this was criticised as an over-coloured picture of savagery in the twentieth century, but Jack and his companions found its material in the islands of the Pacific. Several times he wrote directly following experiences, instead of making notes as he usually did.

It seemed a high tide in the enjoyment of life, but it was soon to end abruptly. All of them had tropical illnesses. Abrasions turned into the huge ulcers called yaws; there were bouts of malaria, with quinine being swallowed like water. Jack wrote of himself as 'the Amateur M.D.' It was part of the sport, an added flavour of hardship and danger. However, in September the fun faded. An unknown disorder afflicted Jack: his hands and feet swelled, his skin peeled in layer after layer, and he lost co-ordination of his limbs at times. He was found to have a double fistula, but the mysterious skin malady was put down to nervous exhaustion. At the end of October he decided that he must go to Sydney to remove the fistula and treat his other illness.

The skin disorder persisted. The Australian specialists were at a loss. In time Jack learned what it had been — a 'sun sickness', caused by his skin being sensitive to ultra-violet light: the same tissue-destruction as affected the early experimenters with X-rays. He remained in hospital for five weeks, and at last accepted that it was impossible to continue the *Snark*'s tropical cruise. He sent Martin Johnson to bring the boat down to Sydney, where she was sold for $3000 and taken back to the Solomons to serve as a 'blackbirder'. After a trip to Tasmania Jack and Charmian, accompanied by Nakata, left Australia on a tramp steamer. Its journey was a slow one, stopping at most of the South American ports and for a month in Ecuador. They arrived in San Francisco on 23 July, 1909.

Both his and Charmian's health were undermined — she was still suffering from malaria when they returned, and had attacks of it for some time afterwards. Throughout the *Snark*'s two years he had been drinking heavily too. The voyage began with a resolution to allow no liquor on board, but Jack drank a great deal ashore. From the Marquesas onwards there was a good supply on the boat, and the rate of drinking increased as they went on. Jack put it down to the tropical heat, to continual entertaining, to the stimulus which alcohol gave when things were difficult. In Australia when he had left the hospital, he resumed drinking as a matter of course. There was no reason to stop now; back at Glen Ellen it became part of every day until, as he wrote in *John Barleycorn,* 'I achieved a condition in which my body was never free from alcohol'.

His affairs were, inevitably, chaotic. Ninetta had been sending out his stories to magazines and newspapers, asking editors what they would give, at the same time as a literary agent offered other copies of them. He had allowed her to recommend and conduct the purchase of a hundred and thirty acres of a neighbouring ranch and the fifteen-acre Fish Ranch to add to his own. The huge barn had been completed and the vast collection of South Sea curios was displayed in it. All of this was more money poured out and fresh liabilities acquired — he took out another mortgage to buy the ranches. Yet Jack himself was full of plans and visions of the 'Beauty Ranch' he would create now. A craze for eucalyptus trees was at its height in California; he planted 15,000 seedlings immediately, and talked of the fortune they were going to make for him.

The answer to all the problems was to write more and more. On his return to Glen Ellen he had nine books waiting to be published, and the income from their initial sales was already received and spent. He set himself a nineteen-hour day, as he had done years before. The stories rolled out, and money came in: $8000 for the serial rights of *Burning Daylight*, $750 dollars each for short stories from the *Saturday Evening Post*. He reiterated that he detested writing, but his thousand words were done by eleven each morning. Jack London's industry is, indeed, almost incredible. Besides his literary output and his business affairs, he received several thousand letters a year and answered every one, often dictating lengthy replies. Part of every day was given to visitors. Jack would see no-one until the afternoon, but from lunch-time onward he was ready for enjoyment as well as work.

Seeking every way to cut corners in story production, in 1910 he began purchasing plots from a twenty-five-year-old publicity man named Sinclair Lewis. The arrangement lasted just over a year; Jack bought from Lewis twenty-seven plots, of which five were used. He paid from five to seven dollars for them, and grumbled a little: 'Frankly, I don't know whether I'm making money or losing money by working up some of those short-story ideas I got from you. Take *The Abysmal Brute*, for instance. I got $1200 for it ... Had the time I devoted to it been devoted to *Smoke Bellew* or *Sun Tales*, I'd have got $3000 for the same amount of work.' However, he looked for other opportunities to buy plots; some were supplied to him by George Sterling.

Very much of what he was writing now was thin in content and cursorily done. What is even worse is that it dealt in national and racial prejudice, and in the cheapest emotional appeals. A possible half-excuse is that he was giving the magazines and their readers what they wanted. They would surely not have objected to something a little better; but the unfortunate truth is that Jack was now letting his own prejudices and Anglo-Saxon fantasies flow. In the South Sea stories which became one of his chief lines after the *Snark* cruise, the recurring characters are masterful white man and child-like, servile native. In *Burning Daylight* the hero is a 'blond beast' come into his own: not saturnine and doomed to destruction as Wolf Larsen had been, but admirable and successful. Indeed, *Burning Daylight* presents a combination of myths. Its hero, Elam Harnish, enacts the dream of which Jack spoke to Anna Strunsky years before: 'to beat the Capitalist at his own game'. Having done so, he throws over his wealth in favour of the simple life and a woman's love — a conclusion which no doubt delighted many readers, but an earlier Jack would have derided it as an opiate.

At Christmas 1909, Charmian told Jack she was expecting a child. She was nearly forty. He was overjoyed at this prospect he had almost given up, despite its importance to him. Charmian wrote of her happiness during the months of her pregnancy. She kept a diary, all extravagant sentimentality and florid phrases; but it would be wrong to jeer. Jack, as she said, burgeoned with happiness. He exuded affection and solicitude, talking eagerly of 'we three'. They went for week-long trips in a horse-drawn runabout, taking only his writing materials. This time, he was sure, it would be a son.

They had planned to have a house built on the ranch, and for Jack the time had come. His intentions had been never less than grand, and they swelled now. The chosen spot was in the ranch's most beautiful canyon, surrounded by magnificent trees. The house was to be called 'The Wolf House'; its materials would all be from the Valley of the Moon — great red volcanic stones and timber from the redwood trees. There would be a library, a music room, a dozen rooms for guests; Jack's own sleeping tower, and a storey to be Charmian's own; servants' quarters; a lounge for men only, to drink and play billiards and talk. 'Jack could not traffic in small things', Charmian wrote. The heart of this vision was now the son he was going to have, and the dynasty of Londons who would live in the Wolf House. Architects were brought from San Francisco, and he and Charmian spent hours mulling over the drawings.

He asked his sister Eliza to come and manage the ranch. She had a small son, but was now separated from the aged and ailing Shepard. Ninetta was still at Wake Robin with her second husband, but on the return from the *Snark* voyage Jack had made a gift to her and terminated her services. Eliza was installed on the Fish Ranch. She was an immensely capable person; more important still, she brought sobriety and stability to the handling of Jack's affairs. Her task was considerable. He had just spent another $30,000 on buying the Lamotte ranch and vineyards — eight hundred acres more, making one vast span of Beauty Ranch. He did not have the money, of course: there was another urgently-requested advance, another mortgage. Charmian recalls a conversation in 1910 when he had $500 in the bank and an $800 insurance premium to pay. 'Doesn't balance up very well, does it? But never fear — *Smoke Bellew* will pull us even with the bills.' The Wolf House, already started, was to cost another $30,000, and Jack was looking for a yacht to sail the inland waterways.

The period beginning with the idea of the *Snark* was the happiest of Jack's life. The voyage, despite its problems and his illness, was memorable. He had cast off intellectual and moral obligations, made his decisions about life. With the return to Glen Ellen, everything seemed to become possible. Uncertainties and frustrations were being pushed deeper beneath the surface. He had the ranch and soon would have his Wolf House; the eucalyptus trees and scientific farming would bring another fortune; he would even give up writing, and complete his boat-voyage round the world. And in a few months he would have a son from his Mate-woman. He felt and talked like a king; he drank, he rode on horseback through his eleven hundred acres, dreaming of the years ahead.

The dreams were about to end. He would never be happy again.

11. Descent from Happiness

The baby was a girl and lived less than two days. Jack was away from Charmian's bedside as little as possible, with Eliza — how glad he was that she was there! — in the background to help and arrange.

He had to break the news to Charmian. From the hospital he wandered miserably through the Oakland streets and into a bar near the waterfront. His version of what happened is that he was taken for a bill sticker and ordered to leave; when he tried to explain, he was beaten up by the proprietor and four of his customers. The newspapers suggested that Jack was looking for trouble. Though his answer was to accuse the reporters of being paid 'to give Jack London the worst of it wherever possible', it is not hard to imagine that he was ready for a quarrel and even wilfully chose the kind of place in which he was likely to find one. He was full of wretchedness that afternoon.

The incident had an outcome. With a black eye to prove he was assaulted, Jack brought a policeman and had the proprietor, Muldowney, arrested. When they went to court, the judge spoke of 'the benefit of the doubt' and dismissed the charge. A letter from a well-wishing stranger then advised Jack to look up certain municipal records; he sent Eliza to do so, and learned that the judge was in fact the owner of Muldowney's premises. Bursting with rage, Jack sent to newspapers and magazines his famous 'open letter to Police Judge Samuels':

> Someday, somewhere, somehow, I am going to get you ... get you I will, somewhere, someday, somehow, and I shall get you to the full hilt of the law and the legal procedure that obtains among allegedly civilised men.

The letter was syndicated all over America. Elsewhere, Jack — and Charmian too — pointed out that the judge was a Jew. No legal redress ever came. But Jack's revenge was obtained in a story called 'The Benefit of the Doubt'; in it, he described the affair in full detail, and the *Saturday Evening Post* bought and published it.

The day after the brawl Jack went to Reno for ten days, to report the Jeffries-Johnson fight on 4 July for the *New York Herald*. He had been insisting ever since he saw Tommy Burns battered so venomously in Sydney that the mighty champion of a few years ago was the man who must stop Johnson's golden grin. (Johnson was reported as saying: 'Why don't Mr London like mah gold teeth? Maybe, as a scribbler, he can't afford them, that's all.')[38] Jack's advocacy created a myth that Jim Jeffries was superhuman in strength and boxing ability. Indeed he had been a fine champion and was a massive man; but he was thirty-five, and had not fought for six years. He was thrashed, and many of the audience wept. Curiously, Jack was not without admiration for Johnson — he had sent home a photograph of him in 1908 from Tasmania. Some of his fanaticism over the Reno fight may be put down to the fact that he was writing for a Hearst paper and supplying to a white public what it wanted to hear. His own sentiments about racial prestige had set still harder since the *Snark*; there is no great gap between the Saxon lordliness of *South Sea Tales* and indignation that the champion of the world is an arrogant black man.

Charmian remained in the Fabiola Hospital for a few weeks. In Reno Jack began a series of daily letters to her, which continued until she came home. They are intensely affectionate and tender; he appreciated that her loss and disappointment were as great as his, and knew the need to give warm reassurances to her. He was more in love with her than he had ever been. She had incorporated herself in all his dreams and projects. As she had been his comrade in the long sailing adventure, she was part of the Beauty Ranch and the Wolf House and everything else for the future. It was a dangerous position, with someone of Jack's philosophy; her place was dependent on the fulfilment of the dreams.

He found the yacht he had been looking for, a thirty-foot yawl named *Roamer*. In mid-October they began a cruise of the coast and rivers. What Jack wanted was to go over the scenes of his oyster-pirate days, redefining his youth against the period he repudiated. They went from Oakland across the Bay of San Francisco; through the creeks and rivers — Benicia, Suisun Bay, the Sacramento and the San Joaquin. Jack found French Frank, a rickety seventy-year-old living in a duck hunters' shack, and sailed past Belmont where he had toiled in the laundry. It was all different now, of course; Jack was a celebrity, and old acquaintances became his confederates in tinting the past. By what seems a strange omission, he did not go to the First and Last Chance Saloon. Charmian, writing in 1920, said she had never met Johnny Heinhold. When Jack's life and haunts of those days had been described in *John Barleycorn*, he received a letter from his crewman on the *Razzle Dazzle*, Spider Healey. The letter said:

> In conclusion the main object of calling your attention to these facts is to let you know the conditions that now exist with the pirates whose names have made you fames, in that book & plan known as 'John Barleycorn'. Johnie Hynold and Joe Viergue are the only ones who accumulated a wad and I dare say buried it like a dog did his bone. To get a quarter from a turnip, is like extracting the same from these men.[39]

Perhaps it was shortly after this that Jack walked into the First and Last Chance, had one drink, and left a five-dollar gold piece on the bar: 'Tell the boys Jack London was in, and to have a drink on him.'

There were to be more cruises in the *Roamer* and, in the summer of 1911, a four-horse driving trip through north California. Before that, they decided to move. They were still living in the annexe to Wake Robin, watching the early stages of construction of their castle. Jack suggested that they take the vineyard house on the Kohler ranch. It was in a neglected state, the surroundings overgrown and the outbuildings damaged. But it stood in the heart of their ranchlands and would allow more space for their crowds of guests. He arranged for the necessary work to be done while he and Charmian were away on the coaching tour, and on their return in September they moved into the house. They never left it.

It was a single-storey wooden house with six rooms; a passage divided it, with Jack's study and sleeping-porch on one side and Charmian's quarters on the other. The centre of its activity, however, was a stone winery building which adjoined the house and now was connected to it by a covered porch. It provided a hall thirty-eight feet long, with a kitchen beyond and a cellar below. One end was furnished for dining, with a throne-like chair for Jack at the head of the long table. The walls were hung with South Sea souvenirs, photographs, originals of illustrations to Jack's books; there were Samoan tapas, a grand piano, cushions and fur rugs on the floor.

Every other space was turned into guest rooms for friends and whoever else liked to come there. At Wake Robin they had been put in Ninetta's cabins and in tents in the grounds; here, outbuildings were converted for more and more people to stay. Jack's letters to enquirers, publishers, socialists, casual acquaintances, men who claimed to have known him or drunk with him, threw out endless invitations to 'come up and visit us' — he had a circular printed, giving directions. Many came and lived on the ranch for months at a time, given nominal jobs and joining the pay roll. Letters flowed in by the hundred, begging for work and cottages; there were convicts, struggling writers, and men who were dying from consumption and cancer. By 1913 he was paying out three thousand dollars a month in wages for the ranch and the Wolf House, a large part of it to people who scarcely or never worked.

Each day Jack sat at the table with never less than a dozen guests. Charmian wrote: 'How he doted upon that board with its long double-row of friendly faces turned in greeting, ever ready with another plate and portion!' He took them on tours of the ranch, showed them the Wolf House and described the splendours to be. There was drinking, of course; and the horseplay of parties at Piedmont ten years earlier now took the form of heavy-handed practical jokes, which Jack never tired of devising. For anarchists there were exploding books and boxes. In one room ropes were fastened to the bed, to be swung upon in the room below and alarm the guest into thinking there was an earthquake.

Some of the guests, such as Sterling and Hopper, were long-standing intimate friends. Many of them undoubtedly came through curiosity; and there were some, like Brett, who had business relationships with Jack and might have preferred less flamboyant hospitality. But the great majority were hangers-on of one kind and another, battening on this unbelievable lavishness. They would applaud Jack's sallies, laugh noisily at the jokes, admire and acquiesce — and go away to talk of his vanity and his drinking. He was not oblivious to their motives. In a letter to one acquaintance he attacked his visitors and petitioners angrily: 'the flotsam and the jetsam that swamp this ranch ten-deep ... Each one pursuing his favorite phantoms. Each one with his muzzle in his particular lard-pail.'[40]

Nor did the ranch prosper. The eucalyptus trees were a failure. In all, Jack planted nearly a hundred and fifty thousand of them at a cost of $50,000. Eventually the United States Forestry Service published a warning that the craze had been ill-founded, and there was no money to be made from eucalyptus wood. The farm land was useless, the soil exhausted. He reflected that the ranches he had bought were all ones which had failed.

> At the moment I am the owner of six bankrupt ranches, united in my possession. The six bankrupt ranches represent at least eighteen bankruptcies ... can I make a success where these eighteen men failed? I have pledged myself, my manhood, my fortune, my books, and all I possess to this undertaking.

He studied agriculture as he had studied examination subjects, cramming facts and theories into his head as quickly as possible, and had Eliza take a correspondence course in crop-raising. He believed that by applying scientific methods he would succeed. The anomaly was a near-worthless labour force, fifty-three strong at one time, without knowledge or inclination. When it was pointed out, Jack was defiant: he was giving men work. He instructed Eliza and the Wolf House foreman that no man who asked for a job was to be turned away. Tramps, men on parole — all were to be fed and paid for a few days at least. When Charmian, from hospital, remonstrated that he was losing money and nullifying Eliza's attempts at organisation, he replied:

> Please don't forget that the Ranch is *my* problem. Netta and Edward never helped me; Wiget never helped me; Eliza never helped me. It was I, when I was ripe, and when I saw a flicker of intelligence in Eliza, who proceeded to shake things down.

What all these various ones have lost for me in cash is a thousand times more than the price of the few meals and beds I've given to my bums. And I give these paltry things of paltry value out of my heart. I've not much heart left for my fellow human-beings.

Though the letter ends with a message of love to Charmian, it signals that happiness had run out. The open-handed cordiality thinly masked an inner anger at everyone about him. The tramps and hangers-on were a symbol not only of the past he liked to boast about, but of his contempt for all the others; the 'bums' amused and solaced him, and deserved their pay more than others deserved esteem. The ranch itself, which he and Charmian had envisaged as a homeland for their personal delight, was becoming a monumental adversary. He wrote to Hartwell Shippey that he was determined to conquer it 'as I strove to master the sea, and men, and women, and the books, and all the face of life that I could stamp with my 'will to do'.'

He drove regularly into Glen Ellen, to the village street where the saloons were, with bells on his horses' collars so that they should hear him coming. Once a week he went to Santa Rosa, sixteen miles away. No one else was allowed to pay for drinks when he was there; the crowd waited for him, calling out 'Hi, Jack!' and watching him wave his wide-brimmed hat in the air. He would go to several saloons in an afternoon, by some accounts consuming a quart of whiskey if he stayed till nightfall. He looked for arguments about socialism and agriculture; one of the attractions of Santa Rosa was finding local dignitaries and business men in the saloons to talk them down on every subject. By the time he returned home he would have bought curios and issued invitations, and drove at top speed up the dirt roads.

There are many descriptions of Jack as he was at this time, yet they are hard to evaluate. He was now past thirty-five; in photographs he is always smiling broadly, confidently posed, a little paunchy. Nearly all those who had met him and sat at the table at Glen Ellen testified to the strength of his personality. He dominated the talk wherever he went; his knowledge, experience and alert mind made him invincible in every discussion. After his death letters poured in to Charmian, affirming him to be 'a prince among men'. Reservations can be made about all of this. It is not a matter of alleging that the tributes were paid sycophantically or in sentimental mood. The age of 'truth-telling' about public figures had not yet come. Those who spoke about him followed the convention of remembering only good things about the dead; others, by the same rule, said nothing.

A different picture was given in the early nineteen-twenties by Edmundo Peluso, who had been a young member of the Socialist Party in Oakland.[41] Harry Young, a veteran in the socialist movement in Britain, met him working as a translator in Russia. Peluso recalled going to Glen Ellen, and finding it a Gargantuan folly where hangers-on and the curious crowded and were fed; he sat among thirty or forty people at meals. Of Jack he said: 'Of course, he was finished then' — a husk of the man he had been, boozing and no longer capable of serious writing. A good deal of arguing was done by Jack in letters; far from showing incisive thought backed by deep knowledge, its substance was assertions and generalisations.

He wrote little that was memorable from then on. He was still producing his thousand words a day, and requesting advances as soon as the terms for each piece of work were agreed. He developed the habit of heralding the quality of the work he was going to do: 'it will be big stuff', 'a terrific winner', 'something clean, fresh, wholesome, new'. It extended to the notes he made for his own use — he would scrawl 'great short story', 'colossal yarn' and similar things on them. In part it was simply brashness, an affirmation that he was at the top of best-selling writers. But the pieces so described were for the most part hastily composed pot-boilers, and he was well aware of it. In 1912 he fell out with Macmillan over some mistakes in the handling of photographs for *The Cruise of the Snark*, and turned to the Century Company. They published four books, but could not deal with him as Brett had done. Ending the agreement with them, Jack made his position clear: '(1) I shall always require heavy advances. (2) The Century Co. seems averse to giving heavy advances.'[42] He sent a telegram to Brett asking to 'resume relations on old basis', and Macmillan published the rest of his books.

Yet, whatever pattern appeared in Jack's life, there were inconsistencies. He was now removed in most senses from radical activities: 'Quite sub rosa, I don't mind telling you that the only reason I am permitted to remain in the socialist party at present moment is the fact that I have never taken any part in the policy of the party.' When he sent money, he reiterated that he was out of touch. He insisted, however, on being known as a socialist. When he was asked to state his beliefs in 1912 he proclaimed himself to be a direct-actionist who believed in violent revolution; but he regarded his active part as done. At rare intervals he stepped forward into some brief involvement with a radical cause. In February 1911, stirred by the revolt in Mexico, he sent to the socialist press an open letter to the 'dear, brave comrades of the Mexican Revolution'. It was superbly-worded and stirring, of the same stuff as his 'Revolution' lecture.

> We socialists, anarchists, hobos, chicken thieves, outlaws and undesirable citizens of the United States are with you heart and soul in your efforts to overthrow slavery and autocracy in Mexico. You will notice we are not respectable in these days of the reign of property. All the names you are being called, we have been called. And when graft and greed get up and begin to call names, honest men, brave men, patriotic men and martyrs can expect nothing else than to be called chicken thieves and outlaws.
>
> So be it. But I for one wish that there were more chicken thieves and outlaws of the sort that formed the gallant band that took Mexicali, of the sort that is heroically enduring the prison holes of Diaz, of the sort that is fighting and dying and sacrificing in Mexico today.
>
> I subscribe myself a chicken thief and revolutionist.
>
> Jack London.

The letter was reproduced widely. Jack gave newspaper interviews affirming his sympathy with the revolutionaries, and followed up with a magnificent story of a fighter among them: 'The Mexican'. It was published almost immediately by the *Saturday Evening Post*, and still stands as one of his most outstanding pieces of work. It was also the end of Jack's burst of fervour. He wrote nothing else about the Mexican revolt. Three years later he became *Colliers'* war correspondent there and announced that he was in favour of the American intervention he had condemned. His articles were sadly but truthfully described as a brief for the oil kings and 'Yankee Imperialism'.

Jack never neglected to respond to the hundreds of aspiring writers who wrote asking him for help. Often the help was material, in the form of money and even allowances. For a time he sent a duplicated letter to those who requested criticisms of their work, saying he could not act as 'a charitable literary bureau'. But after settling on the ranch he decided that he would read every manuscript and encourage writers to send them to him. He replied with letters of advice — one, to Max Feckler, was published under the title 'Letter to a Young Writer'. Frequently he invited the writer to come to Glen Ellen for longer talks, and tried to help him sell his work. When the case seemed hopeless, he sent a copy of Richard Le Gallienne's 'Letter to an Unsuccessful Literary Man'.

In 1912 Charmian was pregnant again, but miscarried. It was the last slight chance there might have been: expectations were not raised, and nothing was said afterwards. Jack began to look towards his two young daughters for affection. Bess and the children lived in the house he had provided; he sent a monthly sum for their upkeep and paid the bills. Occasionally he made visits, or took the children for outings. Otherwise there was communication only when matters of money were raised and, invariably, tempers blazed. Just before the end of the *Snark* voyage, Jack received two letters from Bess asking him to agree to new financial arrangements because she proposed to marry again (she did not do so). He answered with three-and-a-half thousand words of sustained fury, vowing that he would 'fight, fight, fight until there is not a penny left for anybody' before he conceded anything to her.

He attacked Bess for not letting him see more of his daughters. He wanted them to come to the ranch; she told him they were unwilling. As Joan wrote many years later, they were 'pawns in a situation neither understood'. However, when Bess agreed to bring them with some friends for a picnic, the party did not stay long enough for Jack to see them; Charmian in a red shirt and cap galloped past, showering them and their food with dust. Jack promised to build a cottage on the ranch and keep Charmian away from them, but Bess was righteously adamant now. He gave up pleading, and poured out raging, emotional threats:

> The less I am acquainted with my children, the less I shall know my children, the less I shall be interested in my children.

And insofar as you stand between me and knowing my children, by that much will my interest be lessened, and by that much will what I shall do for them be lessened ... Let me warn you that you are playing the part of a dog-in-the-manger when you insist by your past and present attitude in dwarfing my children through their lack of me — and all because Charmian has proven herself a better wife and mate for me than you proved yourself ... Are you a woman? Or are you a mere sexual beast, filled with such sex-jealousy and hatred that you will sacrifice your children and your children's father to your own morbid hatred? Wild Indians, headhunters and cannibals, have sometimes in their deepest depths of degradation, been like this. Are you willing so to classify yourself? [43]

His disappointment and frustration grew and were not relieved by good fortune in other directions. The ranch remained unproductive, giving little or nothing in return for the great sums of money put into it, and refusing to respond to scientific treatment. Abruptly, he announced that he and Charmian were going away for several months — to New York, and then on a voyage round Cape Horn. In New York he had what he swore would be his last drinking bout; he was depressed and unhappy.

The trip served its purpose. Jack had chosen a four-masted barque. They had, in fact, to sign on as crew members because it was not registered for passengers; Charmian was stewardess, and Nakata cabin-boy. Apart from the thousand words a day that could not stop, their time was spent reading and sightseeing. When they had been at sea three months, Jack spoke of something which was on his mind and may have been the principal reason for the trip. He had not been drinking since they left New York: he had proved to himself that he was not an alcoholic. 'It has never mastered me', he said. 'I now know it never shall. There is no danger of it mastering me.' In the future he would drink only occasionally, for social purposes. That did not happen. But in this frame of mind began *John Barleycorn*, the memoirs of his early drinking life. It is a delightfully written book, though Charmian says that she was shocked by the realisation of his 'restlessness and deep-reaching melancholy'; the condemnation of alcohol was, in the end, by a man who knew he could not leave it alone.

They returned to Glen Ellen and the bills, to long sessions about ways and means with Eliza. They had now the completion of the Wolf House to look forward to. Each day they watched Jack's draught-horse teams pulling loads of boulders up the mountain. He pressed Brett for money to hasten the final stages of the work: 'the roof on the stone house I am building is to be of Spanish tile, and will cost all-told $3500.' Another mortgage was taken out. At the beginning of August, 1913, when it was almost finished, Jack brought Harrison Fisher to see it; Fisher said he thought it the most beautiful house in the West. By Friday, 22 August, the workmen had nearly all left, and the cleaning-up was being done. Jack's and Charmian's belongings were to be taken there next day.

In the middle of the night Forni, the mason who had been in charge of the building, was woken in his cabin. The Wolf House was on fire. By the time he reached the canyon the blaze was tremendous; there was no possibility of saving the house. Jack, with Charmian and Eliza, drove across the ranch. He directed men to keep the fire from reaching the nearby forest, but that was all. Everyone from the surrounding countryside came and stood until dawn, watching the red-tile roof fall and the walls become smoking skeletons. Forni and his Italian workmen wept. Only Jack remained calm, as if he had known that the dream would not be realised. Once during the night he said: 'I would rather be the man whose house was burned, than the man who burned it.'

They never knew how the fire started. Jack had been convinced that it was fireproof, and refused to insure it: the huge redwood timbers could be ignited only by determined effort, and the rest was rock and concrete. It might have been a defect in the newly-installed electric wiring. Forni suggested that turpentine-soaked rags, used to clean the woodwork, had taken fire spontaneously. However, all the evidence pointed to an act of malice. There were men nursing grievances, disgruntled tramps, people with whom Jack had quarrelled that day. In the next few weeks he received many anonymous letters accusing this and that person — Forni himself was named. It was taken for granted that the fire was no accidental misfortune, but an outrageous revenge.

There were two directions from which no expressions of sympathy came. One was the socialist press. They had observed the building of the Wolf House censoriously. To them it was a vulgar rich man's castle, appropriate to a Hearst but indefensible for a self-styled 'chicken thief and revolutionist'. They were angered not only by its size and splendour, but by the money it had cost — more than seventy thousand dollars in the end — when the movement desperately needed funds. Jack's answer was that Wolf House and Beauty Ranch were not capitalist possessions financed by profits wrung out of the hides of the workers; the money came from his labour alone. The radicals were unimpressed. The house became the focus of all the resentments which had grown between them and Jack; many of them hinted that its destruction was a judgement.

What he hoped desperately for, as he lay fatigued and brooding, was some word from his daughters. Bess might have instructed them to write, if only a short message of regret; the disaster might bring them to him. There was nothing. After two days he sat up in bed and wrote bitterly to Joan:

> My home, as yet unoccupied, burns down — and I receive no word from you. When you were sick I came to see you. I gave you flowers and a canary bird.
>
> Now I am sick — and you are silent. My home — one of my dreams — is destroyed. You have no word to say ...
>
> Joan, my daughter, please know that the world belongs to the honest ones, to the true ones, to the right ones, to the ones who talk right out; and that the world does not belong to the ones who remain silent, who, by their very silence lie and cheat and make a mock of love and a meal-ticket of their father.
>
> Don't you think it is about time I heard from you? Or do you want me to cease forever from caring to hear from you?

Joan was twelve years old. She answered him at once, begging him to understand the position she was in. The reply angered Jack, but some communication had taken place. He wrote again, and she replied again; they continued corresponding until his death. It was the one good thing that the end of the Wolf House brought him.

12. Denials

1913 was 'the bad year'. Before the fire made its awful climax there were other catastrophes — illnesses and disputes more numerous than usual, losses on the ranch, failures in business ventures. Jack had appendicitis. A prize brood-mare in foal was found shot dead in a pasture. There was a drought, withering the crops and bringing insect swarms to devastate the trees.

Jack's position was serious. He could have declared himself bankrupt after the fire, but he insisted that every contractor would be paid in full. He owed more than $100,000, and was still committed to more expenditure. His income was that of a wealthy man. Apart from the sums his books and magazine stories commanded in America, he was selling all over the world. In 1911 he agreed to terms for the publication of his work in Russia (though, despite becoming a best-seller there, he never received a penny). He wrote to Bernard Shaw, H.G.Wells, Winston Churchill and other popular writers asking in confidence what rates they received from English and American publishers.[44] His earnings in 1913 were in the neighbourhood of $75,000 a year; but he was spending half as much again.

He had four households to maintain. One was Flora's, living in Oakland with Mammy Jenny to look after her. There was Bess's home, and as the girls grew the expenses increased; and Eliza and her son had a cottage on the ranch. These were a burden enough, but they were the lesser portion. The greater was Jack's open hand from which his tribe of tramps was supplied, loans and gifts made to everyone who asked, guests fed and plied with drinks; and his undiminished vision of the grandeur of Beauty Ranch. A few months before the fire he wrote to Brett asking for money. Some was for the Wolf House, but he had just bought 500 more acres, to carry the ranch to the top of Sonoma Mountain, and 'the finest draft horse stallion I have ever seen. It is an imported English Shire, and I have paid $2500 for it.'

Business schemes were continually being put to him. He told a correspondent: 'I average a receipt of 100 gold-mine propositions a year. I average a receipt of at least 100 perpetual motion and other inventors' devices per year, including all sorts of disease cures.' However, he was not immune to temptation by likely-sounding projects: a Mexican land scheme and a fidelity loan company between them cost him $10,000 in 1913. The previous year he had put money into the 'Millergraph', a new lithographic process introduced to him by Joseph Noel, 'a very dear, very old, and very trustworthy friend'; the business failed and the friendship ended.

Early in 1913 he joined the actor Hobart Bosworth in a venture for producing a series of films of Jack's books. Asking Brett for another $2500, he said: 'If the moving picture proposition turns out at least one fifth as good as present expectations, I shall not have to bother you for advances during the next several years.' The first film was to be *The Sea Wolf*, with Bosworth as Wolf Larsen. Trouble began immediately. It was learned that the Balboa Amusement Producing Company also was making *The Sea Wolf*, without reference to Jack — that, in fact, under the law as it was the copyright ceased to exist once magazine publication had taken place.

Jack was enormously impressed by Bosworth's interpretation of Larsen, but thought the film venture could bring him no worthwhile reward until the law was changed to prevent pirating. He joined the newly formed Authors League of America, and circularised all his publishers asking them to look up their transactions with him and assign the copyright of every piece to him. He conducted his own campaign over *The Sea Wolf*, at one time going to New York, where he saw Anna Strunsky for the first time in several years (she was married to the 'millionaire socialist' William English Walling). He was successful in the court action against the Balboa Company. Their film was shown at the same time as Bosworth's, but it had to be re-named 'Hellship' and lost its prestige: a contribution of some importance to the League.

All of this, however, meant more loss and expenditure in 'the bad year'. Jack talked of rebuilding the Wolf House, but without conviction in his voice. Ready as he always was to plunge financially, all the money he could raise was needed to deal with the crises upon him now. He took to the *Roamer* again, taking Charmian and Nakata on coastal trips. His daughter attributes this, his increasing desire for travel, to 'retreat' — the compulsion to turn his back on disappointments and intellectual dilemmas. There may be some truth in that, but the main reason was a more prosaic one. Jack was being pursued and threatened by creditors on every side. From one of the trips he wrote that he was 'doing the most frenzied finance to keep my head above water. I am afraid to go home for fear of having summons served on me. I have been and am being sued right and left.' He told Charmian: 'I'm riding for a fall, financially; but I'm not worrying — you've never yet seen me stay down long. I'll work harder than ever.'

This must have been the prime factor in his decision to report the war in Mexico. He had been offered an assignment there by Hearst. When America sent troops and battleships to occupy Vera Cruz, while Villa and Zapata led a popular revolt, Jack accepted *Colliers'* terms of $1100 a week and expenses to go at once. A theory, founded in a remark of his to Charmian, is that he longed to make good his failures in Japan in 1904. It is much more likely that he seized the opportunity to get away and to make additional money (it was agreed with *Collier's* that he continue his fiction-writing at the same time as the war reports).

He went to Galveston on 17 April, 1914, to receive his credentials and travel by army transport ship to Vera Cruz. The credentials were not issued although the other correspondents had theirs and were ready for departure. Each time Jack went to General Funston he was put off by the General's aide. He was finally enlightened and helped by Richard Harding Davis, the man who had assisted him in Japan. He learned from Davis that the credentials were being with-held because of 'The Good Soldier', an attack on militarism which was now being used on a poster. It had first appeared in the *International Socialist Review* in October 1913, over the signature 'Jack London'.

Jack saw Funston, and vigorously denied authorship: 'I gave him my word of honour that I did not write a line of that canard, and upon that word he takes the responsibility of adding me to his already filled quota of correspondents.' He joined the transport ship. Charmian, who had come with him to Galveston, travelled on a Gulf Coast steamer to meet him in Vera Cruz. By the time they disembarked, the war was no longer on. The American government did not seek to take over Mexico; a show of force was sufficient for its purpose. Jack remained in Vera Cruz, sending articles to *Collier's*, until after two months he became ill and returned to California.

He continued to insist that 'The Good Soldier' was not his. As soon as he was home he wrote to *The Army and Navy Journal* refuting it and drawing parallels with 'thousands of straight lies and canards' about him in his life. When the Great War began he denied it still more strongly, eventually claiming that it was a German invention. The evidence that he wrote it is strong, however. It begins with the language of the piece:

> Young men: The lowest aim in your life is to become a soldier. The good soldier never tries to distinguish right from wrong. He never thinks; never reasons; he only obeys. If he is ordered to fire on his fellow citizens, on his friends, on his neighbours, on his relatives, he obeys without hesitation. If he is ordered to fire down a crowded street when the poor are clamoring for bread, he obeys and sees the gray hairs of age stained with blood and the life tide gushing from the breasts of women, feeling neither remorse nor sympathy. If he is ordered off as a firing squad to execute a hero or benefactor, he fires without hesitation, though he knows the bullet will pierce the noblest heart that ever beat in human breast.
>
> A good soldier is a blind, heartless, soulless, murderous machine. He is not a man. He is not a brute, for brutes only kill in self-defense. All that is human in him, all that is divine in him, all that constitutes the man has been sworn away when he took the enlistment roll. His mind, his conscience, aye, his very soul, are in the keeping of his officer.
>
> No man can fall lower than a soldier — it is a depth beneath which we cannot go. Keep the boys out of the army. It is hell. Down with the army and the navy. We don't need killing institutions. We need life-giving institutions.

The general resemblance to his style is obvious. Some have argued that the style is imitative, that it is bad Jack London; so was much that he wrote at this period. It is true that his manner is curiously easy to adopt. Charmian's books have a good deal of it, perhaps unconsciously picked up as she went over his letters and notes. Edward Payne produced a spiritualist work called *The Soul of Jack London*, claiming to have received messages from Jack after his death;[45] the resemblance is not good, but it is there.

But the most telling inferences are those drawn from his refutation. Jack knew the piece existed before he went to Mexico, and had never disowned it; he did so only when challenged by the military authority. An effective disclaimer could have been made only in the *International Socialist Review*, and he never approached them. Moreover, the *Review* knew Jack; they were presumably satisfied that the piece came from him. It has to be assumed, therefore, that he was the author of "The Good Soldier". No doubt it was written impetuously, like the open letter to the Mexican rebels, to be forgotten when his mood changed. One wonders, indeed, how he would have responded had that letter been the issue. General Funston or another might easily have refused approval to a 'chicken thief and revolutionist' who identified himself with the enemies of the United States. Would Jack have repudiated the words he had used?

In another sense, he did. The articles he sent from Mexico caused astonishment. The *Nation* said: 'That an eminent apostle of red revolution should audibly be licking his chops over millions of gold dollars wrested from its rightful owner, the Mexican peon, by the predatory ministers of international capital, is somewhat disconcerting.' The radical press furiously accused him of selling-out, of being corrupted by more than 'flattering good fellowship' into promoting the interests of the oil men. Jack wrote contemptuously of the peons and their leaders. They followed Zapata, Carranza and Villa, he told *Collier's* readers, not because they cared for land or freedom, but for loot and blood-letting ('a particularly delightful event to a people who delight in the bloody spectacles of the bull ring').

Ironically, before his first articles appeared many radicals believed he was with the rebels. Recalling the open letter and 'The Mexican', they could not imagine anything else. A newspaper published the headline 'Jack London leads Army of Mexican Rebels'. In fact, he was drinking Bacardi and writing in praise of the benefits the oilfields were bringing to Mexico. 'The big brother can police, organise, and manage Mexico,' he wrote. 'The so-called leaders of Mexico cannot.' Only an 'insignificant portion of half-breeds' were causing trouble; the enlightened, wealthy, shop-keeping Mexicans greeted American intervention with delight. The 'half-breeds' were the *mestizos*, peasants of mixed Indian and Spanish descent who formed a fifth of the population, and Jack paraded his racialism. In one article he described a Mexican officer face to face with an American one. The Mexican was puny and ridiculous. 'The American was — well, American.'

The Socialist Party of America had denounced the intervention and the oil men. 'The workers of the United States have no quarrel with the workers of Mexico', it said. In *The Masses* John Reed, who had been with Pancho Villa's army, called on radicals in America to support the Mexican rebels — as Jack had done, three years earlier. These reactions might have been qualified by experience of seeing independence movements, later in the century. Had the rebels won, their government would have had to exploit the oil for their own economy, to the probable disillusionment of the peons. However, this was the age when the excesses of naked imperialism demanded indignation, and to find Jack London on the enemy side was painful in the extreme.

Upton Sinclair argued that his turnabout was an illusion, that his views had not basically altered: 'the exponent of capitalist efficiency who counted upon Jack London's backing was a child playing in a dynamite factory.' It was too late for that now. The change had taken place years before, and too few saw what had happened. To some extent Jack had concealed it by continuing to call himself a socialist and occasionally letting loose some paean of revolt. But the wish which held him was for supremacy, to see the world ruled by the fittest and best and to be assured that he was one of them. Charmian tells of his pleasure in imperial history: 'this is the sort of stuff that went into the making of you, white woman, and me, and all of us who conquer ourselves and our environment!'

Other factors played a part. He was unhappy, financially worried, tired; he drank more and more, and was weakening physically. He had become mentally lazy, no longer bothering to look for fundamental causes. He had surrounded himself with people who would admire his intellectual powers without testing them, and either kept away from or shouted down those who might have sharpened his mind; the 'universality' and wisdom over 'the big issues of mankind' that Charmian ascribes to him were, unfortunately, only forcibly-voiced platitudes.

He went back to Glen Ellen sick with pleurisy and dysentery. He spent the autumn on the *Roamer*, finishing a novel which he had said would stand head and shoulders above all his previous work. 'I am almost led to believe that is what I have been working toward all my writing life, and now I've got it in my two hands. Except for my old-time punch, which is in it from start to finish, it will not be believed that I could write it — it is so utterly fresh, so absolutely unlike anything I have ever done.'[46] This was *The Little Lady of the Big House*. It was a love story set against the background of his ranch, badly and floridly written, full of cheap sentimentality. *The Valley of the Moon*, published in 1913, had been criticised on the same grounds, but did not cause such disappointment as *The Little Lady of the Big House*. André Tridon, writing in the *New Review*, connected Jack's decline with the revelations made in *John Barleycorn*. More important, his article indicates how noticeable the decline was:

> I knew there was something the matter with London's stuff. His vocabulary was apparently gone, his imagination seemed to be failing him, he repeated himself frightfully, his stories were becoming as safe as those of any popular novelist. Read *John Barleycorn* and you will soon enough discover what ails him. He will tell you himself, and the tragedy is that he does not even seem to know how far gone he is.

While he was away from the ranch Eliza sent an ultimatum. The bums must go; if not, she herself would leave. He had engaged them one by one, but they were on her hands now, and she was unable either to pay them or to deal with their unwillingness to work. Jack acquiesced without argument. Though he had affected not to care, he knew he was the victim of parasites. After the burning of the Wolf House he had reflected on the likelihood that someone to whom he had given charity was to blame. He had learned that money stuck to palms in every transaction on his behalf in the village shops. He agreed that Eliza was to have sole responsibility for hiring and firing labour, without interference from him.

Jack's attitude to the ranch had changed. It was still his domain, over which he rode dreaming of 'the beautiful things I own'; but after 1913 he recognised that it would never make money. At the outset he had believed that he would rehabilitate agriculture and stock-breeding in California, and prosper by doing so: 'The rancher who gets good stock and who conserves and builds up his soil is assured of success.' Though he continued with occasional bursts of enthusiasm, building silos and a showplace piggery and purchasing animals, he spoke of it as simply an expensive recreation. He wrote to Brett, near the end of 1914:

> It is dreadfully hard for me to get my friends to understand just what the ranch means to me. It does not mean profit, at all. My fondest hope is that somewhere in the next six or seven years I shall be able to break even on the ranch. The ranch is to me what actresses, racehorses, or collecting postage stamps, are to some other men.

At the outbreak of war in 1914 he applied to *Collier's* — he was interested in going to Europe as a correspondent. They told him eventually that none of the belligerents was providing for journalists at the front; indeed, it was possible that the days of the war reporter had ended. Jack had asserted, as did many others, that a big war could never take place. His essay *The Human Drift*, published after his death, gave the view that modern weapons made war a prospect which man 'with greater wisdom and higher ethics' would reject. When it began, he took the English side and raged against Germany. George Sterling was equally carried away. He sent Jack a sheaf of war sonnets he had written; they wrote each other letters echoing 'Damn the Kaiser!'

The National Executive of the Socialist Party of America issued a manifesto condemning the war: the workers of Europe 'have been plunged into a bloody and senseless conflict by ambition-crazed monarchs, designing politicians and scheming capitalists'. The social-democratic parties of Europe had all made similar statements not long before. The great majority were now supporting their belligerent governments, accusing the other nations of threats to democracy and civilisation; many of the Americans later changed their minds. However, none outdid Jack in pure jingoism. He spoke of Germany as 'the Mad Dog of Europe'. Invited to contribute to *King Albert's Book*, an English collection of propagandist pieces by well-known artists and writers, he cabled:

> Belgium is rare. Belgium is unique. Among men arises on rare occasions a great man, a man of cosmic import. Among nations on rare occasion arises a great nation, a nation of cosmic import. Such a nation is Belgium. Such is the place Belgium attained in a day by one mad magnificent heroic leap into the azure. So long as the world rolls and men live that long will Belgium be remembered ...

To other requests for repetitions of his views, he said: 'I am with the Allies life and death. Germany today is a paranoiac.' He told the Pathé Exchange: 'I believe the World War, so far as concerns, not individuals, but the entire race of man, is good ... The World War has redeemed mankind from the fat and gross materialism of generations of peace, and caught mankind up in a blaze of the spirit.' The most remarkable of his statements was one which dismissed the slaughter as insignificant. 'As regards a few million terrible deaths, there is not so much of the terrible about such a quantity of deaths as there is about the quantity of deaths that occur in peace times in all countries of the world, and that has occurred in war times in the past. Civilisation at the present time is going through a Pentecostal cleansing that can result only in good for mankind.'[47]

But he was sick. According to Upton Sinclair, in 1915 he was to be seen 'wandering about the bars of Oakland, dazed and disagreeably drunk'. He now had uraemia, and attacks of rheumatism. He became corpulent. He was five feet nine inches tall. In 1902, at twenty-six, he weighed a hundred and seventy pounds; at thirty-nine he was nearly two hundred pounds, over fourteen stones. The idea of a change of climate came into his head. He and Charmian spent part of January 1915 on the *Roamer* avoiding creditors, and he arranged to go to Panama on a journalistic assignment for Hearst. Charmian, unwilling to stay at the ranch by herself, decided to go to her cousin in Hawaii; when the Panama trip fell through, Jack accompanied her.

They stayed five months, and returned the following year.

Jack spoke of making their home in Hawaii; it was his last place of retreat. He worked at two dog stories, latter-day versions of *The Call of the Wild* and *White Fang* set in the South Seas.[48] It was a curious, uncharacteristic existence — a prolonged health-seeking holiday, lying on the beach in a floral kimono, drinking in the yachtsmen's clubhouse, playing bridge instead of poker. He was neither better nor worse, but very tense. He had begun reading Freud, Jung and other psychoanalysts. He would call Charmian or follow her to read out passages; at times he worked himself into frenzies, and she had to stay away.

During this holiday he wrote what was almost his last political piece. It was done as a personal favour. Upton Sinclair had made an anthology of writings on the problem of society, and called it *The Cry for Justice*; he sent the manuscript and asked Jack to write a foreword. Opinions as to the foreword's quality may vary. Certainly Sinclair thought highly of it, and Philip Foner, writing in 1947, described it as 'one of the most moving and poetic pieces to come from London's pen'.[49] A different view is that it is flaccid and platitudinous, making no mention of socialism and advocating 'service' and 'nobility of thinking' as remedies. Apparently Sinclair's title did not bring back to Jack's mind *The Communist Manifesto*, which he once read, and Marx's avowal that socialists would do away with justice and create a new world instead.

It was warm when they went back to Glen Ellen in July, and Jack decided that they would swim in the pool in the meadow. He ordered Eliza to bring a gang of men to erect a log changing-house with six rooms, and run water-pipes for two showers inside. Under his supervision it was finished in three days. Doctors had suggested that he play golf for exercise; he sent a foreman to find a suitable place for a course, and said he would have it laid out. The Bohemian Club was about to have its 'High Jinks', the summer outing on the Russian River north of San Francisco. Jack attended it. He brought back Xavier Martinez the painter, George Sterling and some others for a prolonged drinking bout at the ranch.

His war-mania was heightened by the sinking of the *Lusitania* during their stay in Hawaii and by the shooting of Nurse Cavell. 'The Good Soldier' recurred, and every mention of it or enquiry produced angry letters from him. Replying to an Army officer in 1916, he came close to denying that he had ever touched politics:

As far as I can trace the history of this, it was originally published and circulated in Germany, and later on was brought
over to the United States, translated and circulated with my
name attached. And from there it has spread over the rest of
the world. All you have to do is to read my books and newspaper work to find that for the newspapers I have done only
war correspondence and prize-fighting, and that in my books
I am hailed by the critics as the father of red-blood fiction.

Divisions over the war had appeared in the Socialist Party. The
arguments and examples of social-democratic leaders in Europe
had their effect; so did sheer emotionalism. A high proportion of
American radicals were Jews or from Germany and Russia. In the
face of differing views among the leadership, the National
Executive put the matter to a referendum in the autumn of 1915.
The question, cutting through partisanships, was whether the party
would expel any elected representative who voted money for
military purposes. Many abstained, but a large majority voted
'Yes'.

Jack was enraged. He promised to go to New York and make
his presence felt among radicals there. What prompted his
resignation was Edward Payne's. Payne had become a member of
the Glen Ellen Local presumably because he was one of Jack's
circle; it is hard to imagine his having ideas in common with those
of the Socialist Party. He resigned not on account of the war, but
because he disapproved of hectoring controversy. Jack read of it in
Hawaii, and dictated his own letter.

> I have just finished reading Comrade Edward B. Payne's
> resignation from the Local, of recent date, undated.
>
> I am herewith tendering my own resignation from Local
> Glen Ellen, and for the diametrically opposite reason from
> the one instanced by Comrade Payne. I am resigning from
> the Socialist Party because of its lack of fire and fight, and its
> loss of emphasis on the class struggle.
>
> I was originally a member of the old, revolutionary, up-on-
> its-hind-legs, fighting, Socialist Labor Party. Since then, and
> up to the present time, I have been a fighting member of the
> Socialist Party. My fighting record in the Cause is not, even
> at this late date, entirely forgotten. Trained in the class

struggle, as taught and practised by the Socialist Labor Party, my own highest judgment concurring, I believed that the working class, by fighting, by never fusing, by never making terms with the enemy, could emancipate itself. Since the whole trend of socialism in the United States of recent years has been one of peaceableness and compromise, I find that my mind refuses further sanction of my remaining a party member. Hence my resignation.

Please include my comrade wife, Charmian K. London's resignation with mine.

My final word is that liberty, freedom, and independence, are royal things that cannot be presented to, nor thrust upon, races or classes. If races and classes cannot rise up and by their own strength of brain and brawn wrest from the world liberty, freedom, and independence, they never, in time, can come to these royal possessions — and if such royal things are kindly presented to them by superior individuals, on silver platters, they will not know what to do with them, will fail to make use of them, and will be what they have always been in the past — inferior races and inferior classes.

Yours for the Revolution,
Jack London.

The letter contains a good deal that is interesting. It makes no reference to the war and attitudes taken to it. Considered separately from that context, it appears as a lucid affirmation of socialist principles against their erosion by opportunism and compromise. Moreover, Jack had previously criticised the party leaders for thinking more of respectability than of revolution; in a letter in 1913 he said the movement in America seemed 'doomed to become the bulwark of conservatism'. Could it be that he held a truthful vision which at this moment rose above his prejudices and passions — that his last declaration was his first, viewing the Socialist Party as it should always have been?

Unfortunately, no. Rather than state disagreement on an immediate single question, Jack voiced the disaffection between himself and the socialist movement that dated back ten years. It is true that the movement had always been short of class-struggle militancy; despite its Marxist scholars it was only a federation of radicals lacking clear objectives, and Jack's criticism was well to the point. However, by putting his statement in general terms he omitted to say what he wanted from the movement and the working class — how they should fight, and against what enemies. Whatever the answer might have been, it is clear that to support Britain against Germany in the war was a vital part of it.

The terms of his letter made his separation even more complete than he had intended. The Socialist Party's division over the war grew; many more left it. But those who agreed with Jack and wanted America to enter the war were the compromise-makers whose radicalism was not the class-struggle kind. The fighters, whose creed was at one with his final paragraph, were the diminishing section which continued to oppose the war. Thus, on different grounds he rejected both sides and any affinity that remained.

13. Sick Unto Death

Jack asked his daughter Joan to live with him and Charmian on the ranch. In his letters he demanded remorselessly that she declare herself for him, and insisted on answers to the questions he put to her: 'You reply by squealing that you are only twelve years old. Dearest daughter Joan, let me tell you that Truth never squeals. Also, dearest daughter Joan, it is scarcely brave to invoke Truth, and then squeal with fright at what you have invoked.' [50]

He went to Piedmont one Sunday evening and presented his proposition to Joan and her mother. After several weeks she answered that she was happy with Bess and did not wish to leave. Jack was beside himself with desperate, frustrated rage. The long letters he sent to her at this time have seldom been equalled for intense vindictiveness. His letters to Bess, violent as they are, are not without a certain knockabout quality as if he relished composing phrase upon phrase to belabour her. Those to Joan, poured from a sick mind denied what it wanted most, are malignant.

He wrote about the training of a colt. One sought to break it of vicious traits, but if it retained them despite the training there was only one kind of end: 'Let the colt go. Kill it, sell it, give it away. So far as I am concerned I am finished with the colt.' He told his daughter he rejected her in the same way.

> You were a colt. Time and fate and mischance, and a stupid mother, prevented me from having a guiding hand in your upbringing. I waited until you, who can dramatise 'Sohrab and Rustum', could say for yourself what you wanted. Alas, as the colt, you were already ruined by your trainer. You were lied to, you were cheated. I am sorry; it was not your fault. But when the time came for you to decide (not absolutely

between your mother and me) — to decide whether or not I might have a little hand in showing and training you to your paces in the big world, you were already so ruined by your trainer, that you declined. It is not your fault. You were so trained. It is not your mother's fault — she was born stupid, stupid she will live, and stupid she will die ...

Whether or not you may die dumb-mad, I know not. I do know that you have shown, up to the present time, only docility to your trainer. You may cheat and fool your trainer, and be ruined by your trainer. I only think that I know that you are too much of a diplomat to die over anything ... If you should be dying, and should ask for me at your bedside, I should surely come; on the other hand, if I were dying I should not care to have you at my bedside. A ruined colt is a ruined colt, and I do not like ruined colts.[51]

He wanted to hear nothing more of her progress at school; he did not propose to send her to university. At eighteen or twenty she would be 'a little wizened, pinched, human female creature'.

All this would be wounding to any sentient adult; its effect on a child must have been frightful. The correspondence continued, nevertheless. Joan had been told to apply to her father for money for clothes and school books. His responses reflected the pressure on his finances. At one time he would complain and refuse small amounts (once in 1914 after sending her $4.50 he had only $3.46 in the bank). At other times he was warmer and more generous, and wanted her to have 'a high mind, a high pride, a fine body, and just as all the rest, a beautifully dressed body'. The position eventually established in their letters was one in which each was agreeable to the other at arm's length — Joan showing, at least, the affection due to her father, and Jack conscious that he risked alienating her if he attacked again.

He and Charmian stayed in Hawaii from March to August of 1916. They were there when his letter of resignation from the Socialist Party was published, with a reply, in the *New York Call*. The reply found Jack's strictures to be couched in such 'vague and general terms' as to be meaningless. His talk about fighting was turned back on him in reminders that he had done little of it since he became a celebrity.

> We can only assure him that, however tediously peaceable
> membership in Glen Ellen may be, the workingmen in mine
> and shop and factory who make up the rank and file of the
> Socialist Party are fighting — not always the sort of fight that
> makes good copy for the magazines or good films for the
> movies — but the steady, unflinching, uncomplaining, un-
> boasting, shoulder to shoulder and inch-by-inch fight ...
> Live long, Friend London, and keep the pugnacious spirit,
> that, when the way to victory has been prepared by the un-
> heralded millions, you may be with us once more on that
> dramatic day. We shall go on doing our best to hasten it for
> you.

He was stung, but made no response. His only public reference to it
was in a short piece accompanying the introduction he had written
for Alexander Berkman's *Prison Memoirs of an Anarchist*.
Berkman had rejected the introduction as insufficiently sym-
pathetic, and, sending it to a radical magazine, Jack wrote: 'they
deny I ever struck a blow or did anything for the Cause, at the same
time affirming that all the time they knew me for what I was — a
Dreamer ... My dream was that my comrades were intellectually
honest. My awakening was that they were as unfair, when prejudice
entered, as all the other cattle entered today in the human race.'
    How ill he was at this time clinically, it is hard to determine.
'Uraemia' is an imprecise term, describing a collection of
symptoms and alterations which may follow the failure of the
kidneys to perform their normal function. He had always been
proud of his 'cast-iron stomach', but now it refused to accept
meals. In Hawaii he was taken ill early one morning, in acute pain
from a calculus. Charmian writes that he had an illness which
'could not be less than fatal if not checked'. However, in the final
chapters of her book Charmian is to some extent making out the
case for her version of Jack's death; she would naturally lay all the
emphasis on disease, and little or none on drink and psychological
factors. That he was a sick man there is no doubt. There is a
photograph taken at the time, showing him in his kimono seated
under a pergola. Charmian's caption says it displays 'the imperial
aspect of Jack London'. The pose is indeed a regal one, with the
garment draped on his limbs. But the face is bloated and lifeless;
the strong shadows make it almost a mask.

Things were not well between him and Charmian. Living with him as he had become must have been extremely difficult for much of the time; one can only surmise the rages and the wounds he inflicted. On the other side, she left much to be desired as a domestic companion. At sea and on horseback she was his ideal comrade. He had worshipped her athleticism and 'grit'. On the ranch or in Hawaii, where drinking and the entertaining of guests were the main activities, she was uninterested and more than a little resentful.

Throughout their marriage she had spent much of her time working as his secretary. She had been anxious to do so at first; as they travelled, it was obviously convenient. She insisted on continuing it even when the volume of work became massive — one reason, at least, was fear of admitting another woman to close contact with Jack. In the last year of his life she surrendered the work to a man: John Byrne, the husband of Jack's half-sister Ida, who had died. Whereas only a short time ago Charmian had accompanied Jack wherever he went, now she refused to go. They spent periods in which they hardly saw each other.

They went back to Glen Ellen in August for the summer sessions at the Bohemian Grove and the Sacramento Fair, where some of Jack's prize cattle were being shown. Crippled by an attack of rheumatism, he was unable to go to the Fair. Though the cattle won prizes, misfortunes haunted the ranch. The pigs had all died from pneumonia — caught, it was said, through living on stone floors in their palatial piggery. In October the magnificent English shire horse died. Another favourite horse became rheumaticky and useless. Indeed, the entire expenditure on heavy horses was being revealed as an error. Jack had believed his breeding scheme would remedy a shortage and rehabilitate the draught-horse; instead, horses were being replaced by motor tractors.

In addition, he was involved in a legal wrangle over a dam he had built on a hillside. The complainants were Ninetta and Edward Payne. Contending that the dam would divert water which they needed, they gathered support from neighbours and applied for an injunction to remove it. Jack had to spend days in court. At the end of one session he arrived home in a state of collapse. He was now having drugs to relieve pain, and their combination with other symptoms and drink produced bouts of self-pity alternating with quarrelsomeness. He would snap up any pretext to start an argument, work himself into a fury, then lapse into sheer misery.

In elated moods he would make new plans for books, for the ranch, for him and Charmian. He was going to get a three-topmast schooner after the war; with a grand piano, a big launch and a touring car, a doctor and servants on board, they would sail round the world for years. He bought an enormous fireproof safe to store his papers in and had it built into the chimney-wall of their house. Some more acres nearby were for sale; he spoke of buying them, building a school and a general store, establishing a self-sufficient community on the ranch.

Upton Sinclair's wife, Craig, heard the gossip about Jack. She said to her husband: 'I feel that he's in trouble. I think you ought to go and see him.' Sinclair wrote to George Sterling, who replied advising him to stay away.[52] Sterling had ceased to go to Glen Ellen. He found Jack a stranger, and even he could not endure the drunken rituals. Yet his visitors at times experienced the old warmth and charm, and sat listening while Jack read aloud from Percy's *Reliques of Ancient English Poetry*. He bought boxes of gramophone records, mostly operatic, and would sit for hours in the glass porch of the house while his servant played one after another.

No-one was more aware, and more frightened, of his mental disarray than Jack himself. He did nothing to check his physical ailments — his stomach continually rejected the masses of rich food he crammed into it; but he read books and articles on psychoanalysis compulsively. Charmian was both the object of his frenzies and the recipient of his fears. That he did not consult the doctors who attended him for other matters was, undoubtedly, because he was afraid they might confirm he was going mad. Tormented, he confided in Eliza; she had to promise that if he went insane she would take care of him and not let him be put in an institution. He underlined heavily a half-sentence in Dr Beatrice Hinkle's introduction to Jung's *Psychology of the Unconscious*: 'the character and intelligence which makes it possible for him to submit himself to a facing of his naked soul, and to the pain and suffering which this entails.' The lonely boy had never been other than a lonely man. Eliza had once told him: 'Jack, you are the loneliest man in the world. The things your heart wanted, you've never had.' He had always talked of death and asserted the right to suicide. Talking to a magazine editor at the ranch one afternoon, after proposing plans for the future, he said: 'There's always the Noseless One close by.' Now he sat brooding over his life, perhaps desperate with fear.

On 21 November, 1916, he did not go out all day and slept in the afternoon. In the early evening Eliza came to the house to talk about ranch affairs. Jack went over his idea of founding a community. He became highly animated, and kept the conversation going until after supper-time; when Eliza had gone he refused his supper and continued telling Charmian excitedly all the things he would do. Then his energy exhausted itself and he became argumentative, baiting her in search of a quarrel. This too passed. He put two trays of reading matter on the table, and the green eye-shade he wore for working. They sat for an hour, until Jack said he was tired and would go to bed.

Charmian went for a walk. When she returned at about nine, the light in Jack's room was still burning. He always lay propped up by pillows, writing and reading until he was ready to sleep. At the suggestion of his London agents, Hughes Massie, he was writing an outline for a book on his life as a writer. On his bedside tablet he scribbled:

Socialist autobiography
Martin Eden and Sea Wolf, attacks on Nietzschean philosophy, which even the socialists missed the point of.

In late autumn of 1916, when Adamson Bill (8 hrs for Railroad Brotherhoods) rushed at last tick of the sixtieth second of the twelfth hour, through Congress and Senate and signed by President Wilson, agreed with my forecast of favoured unions in Iron Heel.

Novel
Historical novel of 80,000 words — love — hate — primitiveness. Discovery of America by the Northmen — see my book on same, also see Maurice Hewlett's 'Frey and His Wife'. Get in interpretation of the genesis of their myths, etc., from their own unconsciousness.

He wrote a short letter to Joan.

Dear Joan,

Next Sunday, will you and Bess have lunch with me at Saddle Rock, and, if weather is good, go for a sail with me on Lake Merrit.

If weather is not good, we can go to a matinee of some sort.

Let me know at once.

I leave Ranch next Friday.

I leave Calif. Wednesday following.

Daddy

He put the letter in the basket for his servant to post next day. He read for a little while; the book was *Around Cape Horn, Maine to California in 1852, Ship James W. Paige.* At about the time Charmian was returning to the house he laid a dead match between the pages to mark his place, and went to sleep.

Nakata had left them at the end of 1915 to go to college. Before leaving, he had trained a new Japanese boy named Sekiné. The boy went to call Jack at eight o'clock the next morning, and rushed to Eliza crying that something was the matter. Eliza ran to Jack's sleeping porch. His laboured breathing could be heard outside; he was lying doubled up, his face purple and swollen. She tried to telephone for a doctor, found the phone out of order, and roused Charmian. The symptoms were of poisoning — Jack had shown something like them some weeks previously. They forced strong coffee down his throat and produced a little reaction. John Byrne drove the eight miles to Sonoma and brought back two doctors. The telephone worked again; they sent for two more doctors.

The struggle for Jack's life went on all day. They sat him upright on the edge of the bed; two ranch men hauled him to his feet. Charmian held him by the shoulders, shook him, yelled in his face to try to obtain a response. The doctors gave an antidote, washed out his stomach, tried massage and stimulants. In the middle of the morning someone came running with the news of a fresh calamity on the ranch — the dam had broken. One of the doctors tried to rouse him by telling him: 'Wake up! The dam has burst! Wake! Man! Wake!' Lying on the bed, Jack heard. For half a minute he beat slowly on the mattress with his fist. There was nothing else. He was carried across to Charmian's porch and put on the couch there, and in the evening he died.

As with the burning of the Wolf House, there is likelihood but no certainty over the cause of his death. There were two empty vials which had contained morphine sulphate with atropine sulphate, and one of the papers at the bedside had figures on it calculating doses and overdoses. One doctor had no doubt that Jack had committed suicide. It was possible that he had taken an overdose by mistake, perhaps while in acute pain from the stone in his kidney. Charmian pressed the doctors for the benefit of the doubt, to attribute Jack's death to illness alone. They were charitable and did so: the announcements to the press gave the cause 'uraemia following renal colic'. His friends never believed that it was anything other than suicide.

He had made clear his wish to be cremated when he died. His body was taken to Oakland, accompanied by Eliza; Charmian remained at Glen Ellen. Bess and the two girls attended the funeral, where Edward Payne — described as 'Reverend' — gave an address and a poem written by George Sterling was read. The following day Sterling and Bess's brother-in-law brought the urn containing Jack's ashes to the ranch. He had once said he wanted to be buried on the Little Hill a quarter of a mile from the Wolf House, and have a red boulder from the ruins for a gravestone. They took the urn there and put it in the ground, and the boulder was rolled through the surrounding pine trees.

Messages and letters flooded in upon Charmian. The hundreds who sent them from all over the world did not know or care about contradictions and changes. To them, Jack was the spirit of youth. He had come from the working class, fought and adventured; he had told marvellous stories and cried out fearlesssly for revolution; he was handsome and strong, and he had died still young. A girl wrote from Sweden: 'I liked him most of all the authors and men on the earth. I sat in the school, when a fellow student sent me the message on a piece of paper: 'Jack London år död'. I heard nothing more about that lesson.' In America, Mrs Luther Burbank called to a merry group of young people: 'Don't laugh! Jack London is dead.'

The radical press was generous, overlooking everything unfavourable and attributing his resignation from the Socialist Party to illness. *The Masses* said he had brought 'the pulse of revolution' into popular literature; his early speeches and writings were recalled and quoted. The *International Socialist Review* published a poem which began:

> Our Jack is dead!
> He who arose from us
> And voiced our wrongs;
> Who sang our hopes,
> And bade us stand alone,
> Nor compromise, nor pause;
> Who bade us dare
> Reach out and take the world
> In our strong hands.

What Charmian calls 'the most lofty eulogy' was a sermon by a clergyman in Berkeley: 'If Jack London had had faith, what a great preacher he would have made!' He went on to compare Jack with the Old Testament prophets, and to speak of his influence on 'the social and spiritual life of his time'. In reviewing the last phase of Jack's life, several hints were dropped by relations and friends that he was on the way to forsaking materialism and recognising religious or supernatural truths. His sister Eliza thought so. Certainly, in his introspection and his frantic search for a key to the malaise of his mind, he may have grasped at many possibilities. Charmian records her astonishment when he found, in Dr Hinkle's introduction to Jung, 'some sort of inkling of free will' — the antithesis of his belief in determinism and 'the law'.

There is no evidence that Jack ever changed from the conviction he stated in a letter to Ralph Kasper in 1914: 'I am a hopeless materialist. I see the soul as nothing else than the sum of the activities of the organism plus personal habits, memories, and experiences of the organism, plus inherited habits, memories, experiences of the organism. *I believe that when I am dead, I am dead. I believe that with my death I am just as much obliterated as the last mosquito you or I smashed.*' In his immediate circle, however, there were always hopes of something different, and a consequent readiness to note any apparent departure. Spiritualism was still popular; besides Ninetta and Edward, Eliza had a leaning towards it and believed keenly in telepathy. Nor did Charmian altogether exclude such ideas — her romantic streak was too strong. Her biography of Jack is concluded by two long horoscopes: a strange mixture of ironies, in view of her unwillingness to acknowledge that he was Professor Chaney's son.

Jack London's last political statement was a letter to a newly formed political party. At the end of August 1916 the Workers' Socialist Party sent him their first manifesto. On 21 September, two months before he died, he wrote to them:

> Please read my resignation from the Socialist Party and find that I resigned for the same reasons that impel you to form this new party.
>
> I was a member of the Socialist Labour Party. I gave a quarter of a century of the flower of my life to the revolutionary movement only to find out that it was as supine under the heel as it was a thousand centuries before Christ was born.
>
> Will the proletariat save itself? If it won't it is unsaveable.
>
> I congratulate you and wish you well on your adventure. I am not bitter. I am only sad that within itself the proletariat seems to perpetuate the seeds of its proletariat.

Did he comprehend what they said, or what he was saying himself? The Workers' Socialist Party repudiated reformism, syndicalism, direct action, and any form of compromise with the capitalist system; it stood for the establishment of socialism by a parliamentary revolution; and it opposed the war. Perhaps Jack's attention was caught by one phrase alone in its principles — the emancipation of the working class 'must be the work of the working class itself'.

The Workers' Socialist Party was an offshoot of the Socialist Party of Great Britain formed in London in 1904. At the time when Jack was in the East End writing *The People of the Abyss*, Hunter and his other companions were preparing to leave the Social Democratic Federation and found the new party; its socialist principles were those he now approved. The possibility remains that this was the socialism he had always recognised, after all. If that is so, he can be seen as a man continually diverted by his emotions, by passing ideas, by the lure of the kind of life he thought he wanted. We shall never know. Many years later, in 1944, the Workers' Socialist Party published his letter in *The Western Socialist* and commented: 'Though not understanding the principles he endorsed, he was imbued with a working class viewpoint.'[53] That is a comprehensive epitaph.

Jack's will named Eliza Shepard and Charmian's cousin William Growall as his executors. He made provision for his daughters and Bess and his mother, but not generously, and added: 'Whatever additional may be given them shall be a benefaction and a kindness from Charmian K. London and shall arise out of Charmian K. London's goodness and desire.' Apart from some trifling provisions, everything was hers:

> The reason that I give all my estate to Charmian K. London, with exceptions noted, is as follows: Charmian K. London, by her personal fortune, and, far more, by her personal aid to me in my literary work, and still vastly far more, by the love, and comfort, and joy, and happiness she has given me, is the only person in this world who has any claim or merit earned upon my estate. This merit and claim she has absolutely earned, and I hereby earnestly, sincerely, and gratefully accord it.

The liabilities were huge, of course, but Jack's chronic inability to keep up with them arose to an almost unbelievable extent from his mode of living. Eliza said that during the time she kept his accounts, half the money he earned was given to other people or consumed in hospitality; the addition of the wages paid to 'flotsam and jetsam' on the ranch took the figure up to nearly two-thirds of his income. With the prodigal spending in pursuit of any and every fancy ended as well, it was possible for a business-like person to aim at stability with hopes of achieving it in a relatively short time. The income from sales of Jack's books in America was still high, and at his death several were still unpublished.

Helped by Eliza, Charmian handled Jack's estate with a capability which is the more remarkable when one remembers she had been allowed no previous participation in his affairs. The wild hand-outs and entertainment stopped as a matter of course. She felt no obligation towards his dependents — indeed, the terms of his will confirmed her alienation from them — and chose carefully among his friends. She arranged with Brett for three of the books Jack had left to appear as soon as possible, to discharge debts and mortgages, and had her own *Jack London in Hawaii* published. After the war ended in 1918, the demand for his books in other countries grew bigger than ever before. She visited London, where

Mills and Boon were bringing out an almost complete collection. Mr Edmund Cork of Hughes Massie, his agents, remembers her as a middle-aged woman full of vitality, filling the office with her presence and her vigorous insistence on everything being right.

Above all, she made it her concern to keep the Jack London legend alive for as long as she lived. The 250,000 words of her biography were written less for the truth-seekers than for all those who thought him 'a symbol of youth and heroic courage'. She rejoined the Socialist Party of America, to uphold his views and sustain a Jack London tradition. In 1917 she and Sterling appeared at the party's convention and joined with W.J.Ghent, Upton Sinclair, John Spargo, Walling and others to urge support for the war which America had now entered:[54] the stand Jack would have taken. The 'Beauty Ranch', reorganised on a manageable scale, was preserved for visitors. Later, Charmian converted it to a 'dude ranch'. She was always supported comfortably by the sales of Jack's books all over the world. On her death in 1955 the rights passed to Eliza's son, Irving Shepard, and when he died in 1975 his son Milo became the literary executor of the London estate. Part of the ranch became a state park, but over a thousand acres of it still belong to the Shepard family.

Joan London grew up free from the shadow of her father to become an outstanding figure in the radical political movement. Her study of him is written from a deeper understanding of society than he ever possessed. It describes the conflicts between labour and capital in his lifetime and places him — in marxist fashion — in that setting. She died in 1971. Her last work was *So Shall Ye Reap*, a study of the struggles of Californian farm workers.

George Sterling, minor poet, bohemian and alcoholic, died ten years after Jack. His wife Carrie, existing in her own kind of despair, committed suicide. Between his drinking bouts Sterling was miserable and humiliated. In that state he went to the Bohemian Grove, where he and Jack had caroused so often, and swallowed potassium cyanide. Upton Sinclair, writing of the Sterlings and Jack, says: 'I have a photograph of these three, sailing on a boat in San Francisco bay; it is a lovely picture of three handsome, talented, youthful people. Think: all three of them were to take their own lives!'

Among socialists, Jack London's name still gives a feeling of vigour which strangely transcends the knowledge that he was — at least — erratic. A great many people, of both his own generation and subsequent ones, have refused to believe in his racism and chauvinism. When Charles Lestor[55] lectured on Jack London a young man in the audience stood up and read out some of Jack's statements about the first world war. Lestor said they were not believable of the man he remembered: 'They may say he said those things. I *know* Jack would never betray the working class!' Jim Graham,[56] another man who learned his marxism in North America in the early years of the century, made the same reply. Asked about the white man's supremacy and the war, he said: 'I am certain that Jack *would* not ... I hope you will understand.'

Few men have retained this kind of esteem, their failings denied and their merits magnified, fifty years after their deaths; in politics particularly. In part, Jack's early death is responsible. Despite his great output, he never reached the stage where his main tendencies solidified and made his views predictable. Instead, there is a collection of threads, evoking surmises as to their weight and where they would lead. The studies of him that have appeared are all partial, dealing with facets rather than attempting the man as a whole. However, his life was complete as if he had lived eighty years instead of forty. Its various aspects are of a personality whose strengths and weaknesses alike were invited to over-expression by the hurly-burly of the time. It is possible to regard them all, and still feel affection as for a problematic friend.

14. The Materials of Fame

Jack London's books have not been taken seriously as literature. At best, he is seen as an enjoyable but unimportant writer, and his work is frequently treated with contempt. In *Intellectual America* Oscar Cargill refers to him, Upton Sinclair and Dreiser as 'witless, heavy-handed progeny' of earlier realist writers like Frank Norris. Later in the same book Cargill says there is little indication that Jack London and others of his school knew 'or cared to know' what 'the genuine primitive' was. Other critics acknowledge his popularity, but discount it on literary grounds.

Such judgements have not deterred readers of Jack London's books but often create a kind of guilt over reading them: the right to triviality is claimed, a little defiantly. However, it is not uncommon for literary criticism to forget what literature is. Most popular fiction is essentially ephemeral, having no virtue beyond meeting some need of the hour. When further merits are claimed, they have a habit of fading away when the hour has gone. There are no readers of Marie Corelli and A.S.M.Hutchinson today, and no critics urging that they should be read. But if a writer continues to give satisfaction to large numbers of people for a long enough period, he becomes entitled to a place of respect in literature. The needs he meets have been shown to be not transient. It is sixty years since Jack London died, and seventy since his major books were written. Most of them are reprinted throughout the literate world. He cannot be dismissed.

The most obviously striking thing about his work is its quantity. His first book was published in 1900. Including the seven which were published posthumously, by 1916 he had produced 50 books: an average persistently maintained of more than three a year. In addition he made outlines and notes for several more, and half-wrote *The Assassination Bureau* (it was completed by Robert L. Fish and published in 1963). Many of the books are not particularly long. The volumes of short stories are mostly about 50,000 words altogether; some other works — *The Call of the Wild, The Scarlet Plague, The Game* — are barely long enough to be considered novels. By the normal standards of fiction writing Jack's output would be represented in thirty-odd books instead of fifty. That is stilll a notable product of sixteen years' work. If his journalism is added, it approximates to his thousand words every day throughout those years.

Something like a third of the work does not come in for consideration from any point of view. It is doubtful if anyone today reads the South Sea stories or *Hearts of Three. The Cruise of the Dazzler* and *Tales of the Fish Patrol* are schoolboy yarns; *A Daughter of the Snows, The Abysmal Brute* and *The Little Lady of the Big House* have interest only for students of Jack London. These and a few others were produced for the market, with little to commend them other than his reputation and no claim on posterity. The three plays he wrote — *Scorn of Women, Theft* and *The Acorn Planter* — were all unsuccessful, and most people do not even know of their existence.

What is remarkable about the two-thirds of Jack's work on which his popularity rests is the extent to which it was ahead of the taste or the mood of his time. He achieved fame quickly as a writer of vigorous, lucid adventures in the frozen north and at sea. With this reputation as a story-teller established, nothing he wrote was likely to be rejected. Nevertheless, the fact is that the Jack London books which are the most widely read and esteemed today were all doubtful properties when they were published. *The Call of the Wild* and *The People of the Abyss* were successful against expectations. *The Iron Heel, The Road, Martin Eden* and *The Star Rover* (*The Jacket*) were received either coolly or with actual disparagement. One reason why Charmian says little about the last four is that they were still uncelebrated at the time she wrote her biography. Yet without these he would not be famous: known perhaps as an excellent short-story writer, but without major works to his credit.

The reason for doubting whether the public in 1903 would find *The Call of the Wild* acceptable has been noted — its departure from the convention of sentimentality in animal stories. Leaving aside *The Iron Heel,* because it is a special case in every sense, something similar can be said of the other books that either did not expect or did not find favour in Jack's lifetime. *The Road* and *The Jacket* both describe prison life in horrific terms. That, indeed, is the fascination of *The Jacket.* Its historical fantasies vary from the ordinary to the wishy-washy, but the background of the punishment cell grips the reader's imagination. In the early nineteen-hundreds this was fundamentally unsuitable material. A sentimental account of a prison episode, such as Wilde's in *The Ballad of Reading Gaol,* was thought sufficiently daring as the alternative to Dickensian pictures of the wicked receiving their deserts. In showing the brutality of prisons, with more than an implication that justice was a sham anyway, Jack London was a generation in advance of his time.

Martin Eden was disliked for its pessimism, the hero's inability to be happy. Having overcome the odds against him, he finds himself without a creed or a relationship he can trust. Half a century later, in a popular literature without happy endings, the theme was unexceptional and comprehensible; it was acceptable in the nineteen-twenties; but in pre-1914 America it suggested only unhealthy introspection. Likewise, attacks on middle-class conduct and the success-myth were to become fashionable later. When *Martin Eden* was published, their effect was to alienate the magazine- and novel-reading public. Why should a young man with the world at his feet be contemptuous of society and success, and finally decide on suicide?

Jack London's themes were taken directly from his own experiences, and his treatment of them took no account of being 'nice'. Many of his stories are autobiographical, narrating incidents in his life either openly in the first person, as in *The Road* and *John Barleycorn,* or with slight disguises of names and circumstances. Not infrequently he used the names of people he had known in a way which would be unthinkable to libel-haunted English writers. Ernest Everhard is one example, though he borrowed the name alone without otherwise involving the cousin he had once met. In several other cases he used a person whole, as it were, under the person's own name. From his Klondike days there were Elam Harnish, the hero of *Burning Daylight*; Father Roubeau, the priest in *The Son of the Wolf*; and, perhaps most remarkable of all, Freda Moloof. Appearing as a good-natured whore in 'Scorn of Women', she was a dancer whom Jack had known in Dawson City; when he found her living in San Francisco, he presented her with a copy of the book.

His stories appear to be true. In matters of detail they undoubtedly were true. At times when he was challenged over authenticity he was always able to reply with the certainty of first-hand experience. In 1909 he wrote answering an article called 'The Canada Fakers' that had appeared in the journal *Canada West*. A characteristic part of his letter runs:

> You object to my use of the dog-driver's command of 'mush on'. My northland stories are practically all confined to the Klondike and to Alaska, and there the only phrase used as a command for the dogs to get up, to go on, to move, is 'mush on'. There is no discussion about this fact. There is no man who has been in Klondike or Alaska but who will affirm this statement of mine.

To a Klondike acquaintance he wrote: 'Yes, Buck was based upon your dog at Dawson and of course Judge Miller's place and Judge Bond's — even to the cement swimming tanks and the artesian well.'[57]

Yet the use of existing people and true events is not in itself realism. The fact is that Jack London's stories have their persistent appeal because, ultimately, they are not realistic at all: they are romantic fantasy. It is not just the case that they bring a world of distant excitement to town-dwellers; the world is adapted to be as the reader wants it, rather than as he would have found it. The drinking and gambling in Klondike saloons are without the misery which follows them in real life — it is all part of a swashbuckling, virile existence for strong men and beautiful women. The heroes combine superb physique with outstanding intellectual powers. Martin Eden and Ernest Everhard both have muscles which almost burst their clothes. Elam Harnish is 'a striking figure of a man ... he had lived life naked and tensely, and something of all this smouldered in his eyes'. In the Tivoli saloon he puts down every man in arm-wrestling across the bar. The minor characters are in the same mould:

> Graduates of the hardest of man-handling schools, veterans

of multitudes of rough-and-tumble battles, men of blood and sweat and endurance, they nevertheless lacked one thing that Daylight possessed in high degree — namely, an almost perfect brain and muscular coordination ... And in addition to all this, his was that super-strength that is the dower of but one human in millions — a strength depending not on size but on degree, a supreme organic excellence residing in the stuff of the muscles themselves.

The last part of this passage is meaningless. But were Jack's associates in the Klondike really like this? It is unlikely, to say the least. Moreover, the obvious truth about the gold rush to the north is that it was inspired by the desire to get rich — whether or not one calls it greed is a matter of taste — more than anything else.

Nevertheless, Jack London's fantasies are not the same as the fantasies created by most popular writers. He had created them for himself. In practically everything he did in his life, romantic images obscured what things and people were really like. The failures in his personal relationships and his projects were certainly due to this; the idealisation of his experiences in his stories was not simply a selective view from a safe distance, but expectations he had taken into — and, apparently, preserved through — those experiences. One reason is that the experiences of oyster-pirating, the sea, tramping and the Klondike were all short-term, enabling him to feel a member of an exalted and glamorous brotherhood without the disenchanting effects of time. He entered and left them with mental pictures formed by his boyhood reading.

His vision was the same as his readers'. Just as they envisaged a northland full of manly adventures and populated by such characters as the Malemute Kid, so did he. He voiced their feeling that it was far above the life led by the majority of people, that it bred a higher type of man. Smoke Bellew reflects on it:

Alone, with no one to talk to, he thought much, and deeply, and simply. He was appalled by the wastage of his city years, by the cheapness, now, of the philosophies of schools and books, of the clever cynicism of the studio and editorial room, of the cant of the business men in their clubs. They knew neither food, nor sleep, nor health; nor could they possibly ever know the sting of real appetite, the goodly ache of fatigue, nor the rush of mad strong blood that bit like wine through all one's body as work was done.

A number of the stories represent extremes of fantasy. The beautifully-told 'The Night Born' is an example: the sort of sexual episode away from civilisation that most men daydream of at some time.

No doubt many thousands of people in Jack's own time half-believed they might have such adventures, given the opportunity. The legend of the frontiersmen was still potent. Jack's reputation for realism came partly from this belief, and also because his stories had a full measure of toughness. Death is frequent in them, usually by violence; disease, frostbite and scurvy appear regularly, and leprosy is used in several of the South Seas stories. In fact this is another aspect of romanticism. What is signified is the 'law of life' which Jack laid down. It replaces explanation and makes human efforts redundant: 'this is how it is', the author is saying.

Several of the stories are built round this principle. Perhaps the best is a boxing story, 'A Piece of Steak'. Its chief character is a hard-up, ageing fighter who is matched with a rising younger man. His skill just fails to master the other's greater strength and speed. As he walks home, he thinks how narrow a thing it was and how he could have won if he had been able to afford a piece of steak beforehand. The excellence of the story comes from leaving it there, without expressions of sentiment: in time the same thing will happen to the younger man. While we know it is true, there is the feeling that the writer likes the idea of it being true — 'the law' is like God, disposing of man regardless of what he proposes.

This overlaying of romantic concepts on vivid, often harsh, experience produced inconsistency. Some of Jack London's stories fail because of his inability to break through the concepts and perceive what men and women would think and feel in such situations. 'An Odyssey of the North', for all its thrilling pursuit, fails in this way. Even 'Love of Life', one of the most powerful of his stories, comes close to bathos at the end when the man is rescued and among other human beings recovering from his ordeal.

Jack's worst work, the pot-boiler yarns, has been noted. His best is to be found in a number of short stories which establish him as one of the masters of that form. A collection of these outstanding stories would include 'The Apostate', 'The Mexican', 'Love of Life' — the ending is an irrelevance rather than a weakness, 'A Piece of Steak', 'The Night Born', and 'To Build a Fire'. There are six or seven others which are very good by any standard: 'The *Francis Spaight*', 'Under the Deck Awnings'. 'Just Meat', 'The Benefit of the Doubt'. In addition, *The Cruise of the Snark* and *The Road* are collections of episodes which can be read separately; 'Hoboes That Pass in the Night' and 'Holding Her Down' are little gems of writing which is both stimulating and informative.

The reason why these have, on the whole, been denied literary importance is their subject-matter. Whatever the quality of Jack London's stories, they are not taken seriously because their material does not reflect — indeed, it provides an escape from — life as the mass of people know it. This applies not only to the Klondike and the South Seas stories, but to those which are about boxers and tramps; equally, these represent attractive, disreputable sub-worlds of fantasy. Comparison can be made with American writers of the early part of this century — Sinclair Lewis, for example — who, with narrative ability inferior to Jack London's, won critical praise for their pictures of the known contemporary world. Since that world changes, there is no reason why London should not be recognised as a writer of high order. The place for him in literature is much on a level with Maupassant's. His view was too restricted for the place to be a topmost one, but in the field of imaginative story-telling his work cannot be bettered.

Writers are said to stand, or not to stand, 'the test of time'; certainly many books by favoured writers are tedious, two generations after their time. Almost anyone who begins a Jack London book finds himself absorbed by the progression of events and the liveliness of the style. This is the case even when the story is preposterous; there is a quality (perhaps it is the art of the story-teller) which makes heavily melodramatic incidents seem valid. Consider the well-known episode in *The Iron Heel* when Everhard introduces the matter of Jackson's arm. He addresses the mill-owner's daughter:

' ... the gown you wear is stained with blood. The food you eat is a bloody stew. The blood of little children and of strong men is dripping from your very roof-beams. I can close my eyes, now, and hear it drip, drop, drip, drop, all about me.'

And suiting the action to the words, he closed his eyes and leaned back in his chair. I burst into tears of mortification and hurt vanity. I had never been so brutally treated in my life. Both the Bishop and my father were embarrassed and perturbed.

The statement about blood dripping might have been made on a platform or in a pamphlet, but it is impossible to imagine this conversation actually taking place and producing the effects described. What is more, the one-armed Jackson passes the window at once, as if the cue has been given for him to appear. Yet the episode moves on so quickly, unveiling such recognisable truths about conditions in industry, that the reader will accept the idea not only of Everhard's making such a speech but of the girl's consequent immediate conversion to socialism.

Jack's early stories bear the marks of his study of Kipling. The narrative presents no problems, but there are self-conscious discourses in which he can be seen searching for aids to writing well. These quickly disappeared as confidence was gained, and after the first two or three books his style becomes distinctly his own. It is essentially a journalistic style, almost reporter-like when he is describing action. However, it contains another journalistic element which became the worst fault in his writing: repetition. The reiteration of phrases, from a useful device, was turned into a cheap way of obtaining emphasis. It is done a great deal in his letters when he is upbraiding, and can be seen in 'The Good Soldier'. It is a continual irritation in the stories written in the last five years of his life. *The Valley of the Moon* has it:

> Never be without your veil, without many veils. Veil yourself in a thousand veils, all shimmering and glittering with costly textures and precious jewels. Never let the last veil be drawn. Against the morrow array yourself with more veils, ever more veils, veils without end. Yet the many veils must not seem many. Each veil must seem the only one between you and your hungry lover who will have nothing less than all of you. Each time he must seem to get all, to tear aside the last veil that hides you. He must think so. It must not be so. There must be no satiety, for on the morrow he will find another last veil that has escaped him.

This passage is part of several pages re-echoing what could be said satisfactorily in five or six sentences; and there are many more. It is atrocious writing which has much to answer for. For schools of popular fiction in the last forty years have naturally used Jack London as one of their models, noting his verbal devices for 'impact'. Thus the trick of endlessly repeating key words and phrases has become part of the stock-in-trade of every kind of mindless literature — it is one of the characteristics of most 'tough' gangster novels.

However, the writing of Jack's best years is frequently superb. It contains not only movement without reiteration, but some beautiful descriptive passages. *The Call of the Wild* has a series of haunting descriptions of the northland he had known.

> The months came and went, and back and forth they twisted through the uncharted vastness, where no men were and yet where men had been if the Lost Cabin were true. They went across divides in summer blizzards, shivered under the midnight sun on naked mountains between the timber line and the naked snows ... In the fall of the year they penetrated a weird lake country, sad and silent, where wild-fowl had been, but where there was no life or sign of life — only the blowing of chill winds, the forming of ice in sheltered places, and the melancholy rippling of waves on lonely beaches.

These passages drew upon the notebooks he had kept and the imagery formed by his early reading. In later years he became preoccupied with finding plots and situations. He kept boxes of newspaper cuttings, and looked for themes in everything he read and saw. It has been suggested, on the basis of stories like 'Law of Life', 'Love of Life', 'To Build a Fire' and 'The Apostate', that he functioned best as a writer when dealing with individuals isolated in a given background. A wider survey provides no support for this. Rather, it appears that he was dependent on turning up or being supplied with ideas for action against backgrounds with which he was familiar. The effectiveness of the results depended on his attitude to his work — more than anything, on what was happening in his personal life.

Broadly, there are two classes of Jack London reader. His adventure stories have a huge international public; and he is a writer with a special appeal to socialists and radicals. Obviously there is a substantial overlap between these two sections, but it is by no means necessary; *The Call of the Wild* and *White Fang* are classics in Spain, where his political writings are banned. While the radical affection for him is closely connected with the legend that he was, despite his vagaries, a fighter for the underdog, its strongest roots are in the dream of a 'working-class literature'. This has existed ever since the emergence of labour movements. It has never been realised; and of the few writers who came near fulfilling it, Jack London was the only one to achieve fame.

The conception has been of a literature which would be propagandist in content while standing on its own merits in all other respects. Existing literature conveys the values of the established social order; as Marx wrote, 'The ruling ideas of each age have ever been the ideas of its ruling class.' Working-class literature would not only be more comprehensible and satisfying, but its growth would be an expression and a measure of the labour movement's strength. Writers like Morris and Shaw, though they were admired, did not fill this bill. They represented enlightenment and reason, but not in proletarian voices. The need was for writers who belonged to the working class and would express its growing consciousness instead of selling themselves to the status quo.

In this light, a book like *The People of the Abyss* is unique. To anyone who reads it, it is a trenchant and compelling account of the slums of London; but its special quality lies in Jack's standpoint. Technically he was an observer in disguise, but he knew what mattered simply because he had been raised in hardship and poverty. Indeed, the disguise would probably have not been effective otherwise; there are ways of looking, standing and walking that denote class more plainly than clothes. But at the same time he had established himself sufficiently to write confidently, without apology or gaucherie, about the East End he saw.

The quality appears clearly if *The People of the Abyss* is compared with other books describing the life and surroundings of poverty. Engels's *Condition of the Working Class in England in 1844* is the classic survey of slums, making its indictment by sheer cumulation of dreadful evidence. It is written with compassion and indignation. Yet the touches it lacks are the personal, minor ones which in the end are the most memorable in *The People of the*

Abyss: the two men picking up crusts to eat, the young man showing his scrawny arm. On another side there is the most remarkable of all books about working-class life, Robert Tressell's *The Ragged Trousered Philanthropists*. It too is written from the inside — 'Hell, by One of the Damned'. Like Jack London's work, it has been immensely popular among working men. Its failing is that Tressell was not a writer; he did not know how to select, to do away with the superfluous and make his material work to its best effect.

There was, of course, a considerable literature of exposition produced early in the century by the socialist movement. It was most prolific in America: the Kerr company of Chicago published a whole library of theoretical and polemical works on history, philosophy and economics. Though these had a wide circulation throughout the English-speaking world — collections of them are still to be seen on socialists' bookshelves — they could hardly be termed popular works; their function was to further enlighten and supply ammunition to the converted. Working-class literature, it was hoped, would present socialist ideas simply, perhaps dramatically, in real-life settings.

The Iron Heel and *Martin Eden* do this handsomely. What they give, in fact, is a romantic version in which the arguments of the bourgeois are easily cut to shreds. Ernest Everhard disposes of all the difficulties of philosophy with his Texas aphorism 'You've got to put it in my hand'.

> 'Gentlemen, a metaphysician is a medicine man. The difference between you and the Eskimo who makes a fur-clad blubber-eating god is merely a difference of several thousand years of ascertained facts. That is all.'
>
> 'Yet the thought of Aristotle ruled Europe for twelve centuries', Dr Ballingford announced pompously. 'And Aristotle was a metaphysician.'
>
> Dr Ballingford glanced round the table and was rewarded with nods and smiles of approval.
>
> 'Your illustration is most unfortunate', Ernest replied. 'You refer to a very dark period in human history. In fact, we call that period the Dark Ages. A period wherein science was raped by the metaphysicians, wherein physics became a search for the Philosopher's Stone, wherein chemistry became alchemy, and astronomy became astrology.'

Martin Eden is taken by his friend Brissenden into circles where working people talk about intellectual questions in the same way, bringing them alive.

> It was impossible that this should be, much less in the labour ghetto south of Market. The books were alive in these men. They talked with fire and enthusiasm, the intellectual stimuli stirring them as he had seen drink and anger stir other men. What he heard was no longer the dry philosophy of the printed word, written by half-mythical demi-gods like Kant and Spencer. It was living philosophy, with warm, red blood, incarnated in these two men till its very features worked with excitement. Now and again other men joined in, and all followed the discussion, with cigarettes going out in their hands, and with alert, intent faces.

This undoubtedly makes the reader, who perhaps feels there are things he should understand but does not, believe he is being given a key to the mysteries. It also makes them appear relevant to everyday life, and highly attractive. After listening to that discussion Martin Eden is 'as excited as a child on its first visit to the circus', and the reader may well feel the same. Both books, in short, popularise ideas. The same elements are present in *The Sea Wolf*, though Wolf Larsen does not do much more than throw phrases about. Nevertheless, problems of society are made comprehensible and exciting. Alongside these revelations, the personal adventures described in *The Road* become a stimulating supplement. They appear as the exploits of a nonconformist, thumbing his nose at respectability and authority.

In the context of the idea of a working-class literature, the motif of *The Iron Heel* has not been troubled about or questioned very much. It is not far from being an anti-socialist work; at the least, it was written by someone who had changed his mind. The majority of radicals, however, are satisfied that it is 'about' socialism and is the only such book to have attained popularity of the best-seller kind. Whatever its faults, the sentiment runs, we could do with many more like it. Probably that is the great value of *The Iron Heel*, as a type of book rather than for its message. One of Cargill's pejorative phrases is 'a crude sort of socialism, such as Jack London stood for'. Socialism *is* crude. It is the demand of the working class to take possession of its own; the other, refined sort is only an intellectual attitude.

The merit of Jack London's writings about socialism and revolution is this 'crudity' — their vigour and simplicity. It is true that he captured a unique combination of social factors that cannot be reproduced. They included the swift, almost violent transformation of American society; the growth of an energetic but confused radical movement; the technical innovations which brought into being a popular press looking for writers who expressed the aspirations of the time. He can be identified also with a type well-known for a hundred years in Britain but transitory in America — the self-educated working man. Part of his individuality was undoubtedly due to accidents of circumstance: with greater stability in his upbringing, or had he remained at university, he would have been a better-adjusted person. In that case, it is unlikely that we should have the writer who, repudiating the description of himself as a scholar and man of letters, said:

> Before people had given me any of these titles ... I was work-ing in a cannery, a pickle factory, was a sailor before the mast, and spent months at a time looking for work in the ranks of the unemployed; and it is the proletarian side of my life that I revere the most, and will cling to as long as I live. [58]

Notes

1 *Jack London* by Mrs Jack London. Macmillan, 1921 (US title: *The Book of Jack London*). Published in Britain by Mills & Boon.

2 Ina Coolbrith was a leading figure in the Californian group of poets and writers.

3 W.W.Jacobs, 1863-1943, British writer of short stories which are mostly about seafaring men.

4 Letter to Anna Strunsky, 11 February 1902.

5 This description is in a letter from Jack London to Cloudesley Johns, 1 April 1901.

6 This cannot possibly be true. Martin Johnson's home was at Independence, Kansas, over three hundred miles from Chicago. By his own account in *Through the South Seas with Jack London* he was twenty when he applied for the *Snark* job in 1906. Thus, at the time of the encounter alleged by Livingston, he was eight years old.

7 The 'duty' letter was written on 30 November 1898.

8 This incident appears in *Martin Eden*. Mrs Eames tried to have the passage removed from the book.

9 Letter to Anna Strunsky, 3 February 1900.

10 *The Son of the Wolf* was published in Britain under the title *An Odyssey of the North*.

11 Minnie Maddern Fiske, 1865-1932, distinguished American actress who began her stage career as a child. She wanted to take Jack London's daughter Joan on the stage, but he refused to allow it because theatrical life meant 'falseness, artificiality, sterility and unhappiness'.

12 Herman Whitaker was successful. He became well known as a writer for magazines.

13   Joan London was born on 15 January 1901.

14   Letter to Anna Strunsky, 31 July 1902.

15   This information is given in *East End Jewish Radicals 1875-1914* by William J. Fishman, 1975. Flower and Dean Street was demolished in 1975.

16   Austin Lewis's observations were made to Joan London for use in *Jack London and His Times.*

17   This piece is not part of the essay 'The Scab'. Arguments against Jack London's authorship were given by Tony Bubka in the November 1966 *American Book Collector,* and a list of other references to the question can be found in *Jack London: A Bibliography.*

18   *Ten Blind Leaders of the Blind* was published by Charles H. Kerr, Chicago, 1912.

19   This letter is given in Charmian London's book.

20   In section vii: 'Modern ethnology inclines more and more towards such an outlook, and consequently ascribes less and less importance to race as a factor in the history of civilisation. 'The possession of a certain amount of civilisation,' writes Ratzel, 'has nothing whatever to do with race in itself.' Still, there can be no doubt that, as soon as a certain level of civilisation has been attained, this civilisation exercises an influence upon the bodily and mental qualities of the race.'

21   This correspondence took place in November 1902.

22   Though Jack London named 'The Flight of the Duchess' as an intended work several times, it was never written.

23   Letter to Cloudesley Johns, 17 October 1900.

24   Letter to Charmian, quoted in her book.

25   Letter to Carrie Sterling, 29 September 1905.

26   Letter to Carrie Sterling, 15 September 1905.

27   Edwin Emerson Jr. was one of the Californian group of writers. Besides his statement in 1904, it was he who drew attention to 'The Good Soldier' in *The Army and Navy Journal* in January 1914.

28   Bierce's remarks about *The Sea Wolf* were made in a letter to George Sterling on 18 February 1905.

29   'To hell with the Constitution' had been repeated recently by General Sherman Bell, with reference to striking miners. Jack London took it up 'to warn the capitalists that the workers may someday use the same term'.

30 'Love of Life' was shown to have been re-written from 'Lost in the Land of the Midnight Sun' by Augustus Biddle and J.K. Macdonald, which appeared in *McClure's* in 1901. *Before Adam* owed its inspiration to Stanley Waterloo's *The Story of Ab.* Another charge of plagiarism was made over similarities between *The Call of the Wild* and Dr E.R.Young's *My Dogs in the Northland.* in 1909 Frank Harris published in *Vanity Fair* (London) an extract from an article written by him in 1901 beside part of the chapter 'The Bishop's Vision' from *The Iron Heel*, showing that about 1,000 words had been lifted from his piece.

31 Letter to George Sterling, 28 May 1905.

32 Letter to Ernest Untermann, 11 April 1914.

33 *Sailing Alone Round the World* by Captain Joshua Slocum.

34 From the Foreword to *The Cruise of the Snark.*

35 Trotsky read *The Iron Heel* for the first time in 1937. His views on it, stated at length, are given in *Jack London and his Times.*

36 Letter to Rev. H. Rogers, 1946 (*Collected Essays, Journalism and Letters of George Orwell*, Vol. 4).

37 Introduction to *Love of Life and Other Stories*, Elek, 1946.

38 See *The Jack Johnson Story* by Tony Van Den Bergh, 1956.

39 Letter dated 27 May 1916.

30 Letter to Fred Berry, 26 June 1913.

41 In 1935 Peluso wrote some recollections of Jack London in the Oakland Local of the Socialist Party. His name appears in *The Terror in Russia* by Robert Conquest, in the lists of those executed in the pre-war purges.

42 Letter to William Ellsworth of the Century Co., 9 April 1913.

43 Letter to Bessie London, 8 January 1911.

44 Letter to Winston Churchill, Robert W. Chambers, Lloyd Osborne, Owen Johnson, George Bernard Shaw and H.G. Wells, 23 March 1913.

45 *The Soul of Jack London*, Rider & Co., 1927, and Psychic Book Club (London), 1945.

46 Letter to Roland Phillips of *Cosmopolitan* magazine, 14 March 1913.

47 Jack London's statements about the 1914-18 war are given in Charmian's book.

48 *Jerry of the Islands* and *Michael, Brother of Jerry.*

49 From *Jack London, American Rebel*, which gives the foreword in full.

50 Letter to Joan London, 5 September 1913.
51 Letter to Joan London, 24 February 1914.
52 See *The Cup of Fury* by Upton Sinclair.
53 *Western Socialist*, February 1944.
54 See *An American Testament* by Joseph Freeman.
55 Charles Lestor, who died in 1952, was a speaker for the Socialist Party of Canada before 1914 and editor of the *One-Big Union Bulletin* in the nineteen-twenties. He settled in England in 1933.
56 Jim Graham, who died in 1968, was in the Socialist Party of Canada early in this century. Later he was chairman of the Independent Labour Party in Britain.
57 Letter to Marshall Bond, 17 December 1903.
58 In an address to a socialist meeting in Los Angeles in 1905.

Jack London's Works

1. *The Son of the Wolf*, Houghton Mifflin 1900. Published in Britain under the title *An Odyssey of the North*. Collected stories: The White Silence; The Son of the Wolf; The Men of Forty Mile; In a Far Country; To the Man on Trail; The Priestly Prerogative; The Wisdom of the Trail; The Wife of a King; An Odyssey of the North.

2. *The God of his Fathers*, McClure, Phillips 1901. Collected stories: The God of his Fathers; The Great Interrogation; Which Make Men Remember; Siwash; The Man With the Gash; Jan, the Unrepentant; Grit of Women; Where the Trail Forks; A Daughter of the Aurora; At the Rainbow's End; The Scorn of Women.

3. *A Daughter of the Snows*, J.B. Lippincott 1902. Novel.

4. *Children of the Frost*, Macmillan 1902. Collected stories: In the Forests of the North; The Law of Life; Nam-Bok the Unveracious; The Master of Mystery; The Sunlanders; The Sickness of Lone Chief; Keesh, the Son of Keesh; The Death of Ligoun; Li Wan, the Fair; The League of the Old Men.

5. *The Cruise of the 'Dazzler'*, Century Co. 1902. Juvenile Novel.

6. *The Call of the Wild*, Macmillan 1903. Novel.

7. *The Kempton-Wace Letters*. Written in collaboration with Anna Strunsky. Macmillan 1903. Novel and philosophical debate.

8. *The People of the Abyss*, Macmillan 1903. First-hand observation of the East End of London.

9. *The Faith of Men*, Macmillan 1904. Collected stories: A Relic of the Pliocene; A Hyperborean Brew; The Faith of Men; Too Much Gold; The One Thousand Dozen; The Marriage of Lit-Lit; Batard; The Story of Jees-Uck.

10. *The Sea Wolf*, Macmillan 1904. Novel.

11. *War of the Classes*, Macmillan 1905. Sociological essays: The Class

Struggle; The Tramp; The Scab; The Question of the Maximum; A Review; Wanted: A New Law of Development; How I Became A Socialist.

12. *The Game*, Macmillan 1905. Novel.

13. *Tales of the Fish Patrol*, Macmillan 1905. White and Yellow; The King of the Crooks; A Raid on Oyster Pirates; The Siege of the *Lancashire Queen*; Charley's Coup; Demetrios Contos; Yellow Handkerchief.

14. *Moon-Face, and other stories*, Macmillan 1906. Moon-Face: A Story of a Mortal Antipathy; The Leopard Man's Story; Local Colour; Amateur Night; The Minions of Midas; The Shadow and the Flesh; All-Gold Canyon; Planchette.

15. *Scorn of Women*, Macmillan 1906. Play.

16. *White Fang*, Macmillan 1906. Novel.

17. *Love of Life, and other stories*, Macmillan 1907. Love of Life; A Day's Lodging; The White Man's Way; The Story of Keesh; The Unexpected; Brown Wolf; The Sun Dog Trail; Negore, the Coward.

18. *Before Adam*, Macmillan 1907. Novel.

19. *The Road*, Macmillan 1907. Tramping experiences: Confession; Holding Her Down; Pictures; 'Pinched'; The Pen; Hoboes that Pass in the Night; Road-Kids and Gay-Cats; Two Thousand Stiffs; Bulls.

20. *The Iron Heel*, Macmillan 1908. Novel.

21. *Martin Eden*, Macmillan 1909. Novel.

22. *Lost Face*, Macmillan 1910. Collected stories: Lost Face; Trust; To Build a Fire; That Spot; Flush of Gold; The Passing of Marcus O'Brien; The Wit of Porportuk.

23. *Revolution*, Macmillan 1910. Sociological essays and others: Revolution; The Somnambulists; The Dignity of Dollars; Goliah; The Golden Poppy; The Shrinkage of the Planet; The House Beautiful; The Gold Hunters of the North; Foma Gordyeeff; These Bones Shall Rise Again; The Other Animals; The Yellow Peril; What Life Means to Me.

24. *Burning Daylight*, Macmillan 1910. Novel.

25. *Theft*, Macmillan 1910. Play.

26. *When God Laughs*, Macmillan 1911. Collected stories: When God Laughs; The Apostate; A Wicked Woman; Just Meat; Created He Them; The Chinago; Make Westing; Semper Idem; A Nose for the King; The 'Francis Spaight'; A Curious Fragment; A Piece of Steak.

27. *Adventure*, Macmillan 1911. Novel.

28. *The Cruise of the 'Snark'*, Macmillan 1911. Collected articles: Foreword; The Inconceivable and Monstrous; Adventure; Finding One's Way About; The First Landfall; A Royal Sport; The Lepers of Molokai; The House of the Sun; A Pacific Traverse; Typee; The Nature Man; The High Seat of Abundance; Stone-Fishing of Bora Bora; The Amateur Navigator; Cruising in the Solomons; Beche de Mer English; The Amateur MD; Backword.

29. *South Sea Tales*, Macmillan 1911. The House of Mapuhi; The Whale Tooth; Mauki; "Yah ! Yah ! Yah !"; The Heathen; The Terrible Solomons; The Inevitable White Man; The Seed of M'Coy.

30. *A Son of the Sun*, Doubleday, Page 1912. Collected stories: A Son of the Sun; The Proud Goat of Aloysius Pankburn; The Devils of Fuatino; The Jokers of New Gibbon; A Little Account with Swithin Hall; A Goboto Night; The Feathers of the Sun; The Pearls of Parlay.

31. *The House of Pride*, Macmillan 1912. Collected stories: The House of Pride; Koolau the Leper; Good-bye, Jack!; Aloha Oe; Chun Ah Chun; The Sheriff of Kona; Jack London, by Himself.

32. *Smoke Bellew Tales*, Century 1912. Published in Britain in two volumes entitled *Smoke Bellew* and *Smoke and Shorty*. The Taste of Meat; The Meat; The Stampede to Squaw Creek; Shorty Dreams; The Man on the Other Bank; The Race for Number Three; The Story of the Little Man; The Hanging of Cultus George; The Mistake of Creation; A Flutter in Eggs; The Town-Site of Tra-Lee; Wonder of Woman.

33. *The Night Born*, Century 1913. Collected stories: The Night Born; The Madness of John Harned; When the World was Young; The Benefit of the Doubt; Winged Blackmail; Bunches of Knuckles; War; Under the Deck Awnings; To Kill a Man; The Mexican.

34. *The Abysmal Brute*, Century 1913. Novel.

35. *John Barleycorn*, Century 1913. Novel.

36. *The Valley of the Moon*, Macmillan 1913, Novel.

37. *The Strength of the Strong*, Macmillan 1914. Collected stories: The Strength of the Strong; South of the Slot; The Unparalleled Invasion; The Enemy of All the World; The Dream of Debs; The Sea Farmer; Samuel.

38. *The Mutiny of the Elsinore*, Macmillan 1914. Novel.

39. *The Scarlet Plague*, Macmillan 1915. Novel.

40. *The Star Rover*, Macmillan 1915. Novel. Published in Britain under the title *The Jacket*.

41. *The Acorn Planter*, Macmillan 1916. Play.

42. *The Little Lady of the Big House*, Macmillan 1916. Novel.

43. *Turtles of Tasman*, Macmillan 1916. Collected stories: Turtles of Tasman; The Eternity of Forms; Told in the Drooling Ward; The Hobo and the Fairy; The Prodigal Father; The First Poet; Finis; The End of the Story.

44. *The Human Drift*, Macmillan 1917. Articles arranged by Jack London for publication shortly before his death, and published posthumously: The Human Drift; Nothing That Ever Came to Anything!; That Dead Men Rise up Never; Small-Boat Sailing; Four Horses and a Sailor; A Classic of the Sea; A Wicked Woman (curtain raiser); The Birth Mark (sketch).

45. *Jerry of the Islands*, Macmillan 1917. Novel.

46. *Michael, Brother of Jerry*, Macmillan 1917. Novel.

47. *The Red One*, Macmillan 1918. Collected stories: The Red One; The Hussy; Like Argus of the Ancient Times; The Princess.

48. *On the Makaloa Mat*, Macmillan 1919. Published in Britain under the title *Island Tales*. Collected stories: On the Makaloa Mat; The Bones of Kahekili; When Alice Told her Soul; Shin-Bones; The Water Baby; The Tears of Ah Kim; The Kanaka Surf.

49. *Hearts of Three*, Macmillan 1920. Novel.

50. *Dutch Courage*, Macmillan 1922. Collected stories: Dutch Courage; Typhoon off the Coast of Japan; The Lost Poacher; The Banks of the Sacramento; Chris Farrington, Able Seaman; To Repel Boarders; An Adventure in the Upper Sea; Bald-Face; In Yeddo Bay; Whose Business Is To Live.

51. *The Assassination Bureau*, McGraw Hill 1963. Novel, unfinished at Jack London's death and completed by Robert L. Fish.

52. *Letters from Jack London*, edited by King Hendricks and Irving Shepard, Odyssey Press 1965.

53. *Jack London Reports*, edited by King Hendricks and Irving Shepard, Doubleday & Co. 1970. War correspondence and reports, sports articles and miscellaneous writings.

Index

Complete list of
Pluto books available from:
Pluto Press Ltd, Unit 10 Spencer Court,
7 Chalcot Road, London NW1 8LH

In the USA, from:
Urizen Books Inc, 66 West Broadway,
Suite 406, New York, NY 10007

Larissa Reissner

Hamburg at the Barricades
and other writings on Weimar Germany

Compiled and translated from the Russian by Richard Chappell

Larissa Reissner was a remarkable woman and writer, admired by people as varied as Pasternak, Radek, Shklovsky, Sosnovsky, whose tributes are included in this volume.

She was born on May Day 1895 in Lublin, Poland. She was active in the events that led up to the Russian Revolution — as a young woman journalist and propagandist. She was a Bolshevik and fighter with the Volga Flotilla during the Civil War; and with her husband Raskolnikov, a member of Soviet Russia's diplomatic mission in Afghanistan. Her last years were spent in Germany and in the Urals in Russia, recording the eruptions of the new society.

This collection of Reissner's writings on Weimar Germany comes out of her pursuit of the migrating centre of European revolution. She arrived in Dresden in October 1923 as Red Saxony was being overrun by government troops. Retreating to Berlin and the charred lives of a demoralised working class she wrote *Berlin, October 1923*. She then rushed to record the heroic, hopeless Communist uprising in Hamburg, in *Hamburg at the Barricades*, and finally, in 1924, sketched the world of Krupp's Essen and the full horror for the German working class of stabilisation and defeat in *In Hindenburg's Germany*.